Accelerate

• • • • • • • • • •

A SKILLS-BASED SHORT COURSE

ELEMENTARY

Series editor: Philip Prowse

SUE BAILEY • SARA HUMPHREYS

Heinemann English Language Teaching, Oxford

A division of Macmillan Publishers Limited

Companies and representatives throughout the world

ISBN 0 435 28261 1

Text © Sue Bailey and Sara Humphreys 1995
Design and illustration © Macmillan Publishers Limited 1998

Heinemann is a registered trademark of Reed Educational & Professional Publishing Limited

First published 1995

All rights reserved; no part of this publication may be reproduced, stored in a retrieval system, or transmitted in any form or by any means, electronic, mechanical, photocopying, recording or otherwise, without the prior written permission of the publishers.

Designed by eMC Design, Bromham, Bedfordshire
Cover design by Richard Gillingwater
Cover photograph by Frank Orel/Tony Stone Images

The publishers would like to thank *Young Telegraph* for the text "One giant leap' on page 62.

Printed and bound in Great Britain by Thomson Litho Ltd, East Kilbride, Scotland

98 99 00 01 02 11 10 9 8 7 6 5 4

Contents

Map of the book

Unit 1
Tradition
Lesson 1 Family celebrations — 2
Lesson 2 Festivals — 4
Lesson 3 Customs — 6

Unit 2
Sell it to me
Lesson 1 Where to go — 8
Lesson 2 Mail order shopping — 10
Lesson 3 Advertisements — 12

Unit 3
Islands
Lesson 1 Which island? — 14
Lesson 2 Survival at sea — 16
Lesson 3 Skeleton Island — 18

Unit 4
Storytelling
Lesson 1 '... our dream's come true' — 20
Lesson 2 Cindy's crisis — 22
Lesson 3 'I can't live without your love' — 24

Unit 5
Family life
Lesson 1 What size family? — 26
Lesson 2 House rules — 28
Lesson 3 Family roles — 30

Unit 6
Time
Lesson 1 Murder at Château Firenze — 32
Lesson 2 Time capsules — 34
Lesson 3 The Olympic Games — 36

Unit 7
Collectors' items
Lesson 1 An unusual collection — 38
Lesson 2 Collecting information — 40
Lesson 3 'The Collector' — 42

Unit 8
A week of entertainment
Lesson 1 What's on? — 44
Lesson 2 A celebrity guest — 46
Lesson 3 Choosing a programme — 48

Unit 9
The natural world
Lesson 1 Whales — 50
Lesson 2 Favourite animals — 52
Lesson 3 Nature at work — 54

Unit 10
Into the unknown
Lesson 1 The Blue Nile — 56
Lesson 2 Cycling across the Andes — 58
Lesson 3 Organising an expedition — 60

Test — 62
Tapescripts — 66

Introduction

Views of language learning

Create two images in your mind: a large oak tree growing in a green field, and a large jigsaw puzzle of a tree which is partly completed.

What has this got to do with language learning? Simply the images of oak and jigsaw represent differing ways of looking at language learning. For many people, learning a language is like doing a jigsaw: the language is broken up into lots of little bits and they are pieced together, one by one, until the whole picture is built up. Incredibly, despite all the discussion over language learning in the last quarter of a century, this is still a popular view and lessons are expected to contain one grammatical point at a time. The bit of grammar is learnt just like that, and the learner goes on to the next bit. Regrettably therefore, most learners leave their English classes with only part of the picture – rather like the partly-done jigsaw you imagined. Leonard Newmark expressed this well nearly thirty years ago in 'How not to interfere with language learning' (*International Journal of American Linguistics*, 32, January 1966):

'If the task of learning to speak English were additive and linear [...] the child learner would be old before he [sic] could say a single appropriate thing and the adult learner would be dead.'

The other view compares language learning to the oak. It is natural, growing and changing. An oak is still an oak whether it is the mighty tree you may have imagined or a tiny sapling. All trees are unique, yet share similar characteristics. In this view of language learning, learners learn by doing, by using the language in contexts that interest them. Different learners will learn different things from the same lesson – in the language classroom there is no one-to-one correspondence between learning and teaching, or as David Nunan put it at IATEFL in 1994, 'Why Don't Learners Learn What Teachers Teach?'. The differences between the two approaches are summarized by Dave Willis in *The Lexical Syllabus* (Collins, 1990):

'Form-focused approaches see language as a system of patterns or structures [...] Task-based approaches see language as a system of meanings.'

What's in *Accelerate*?

The oak and jigsaw also help us with the problem of what to include in a book or course. When a jigsaw is complete nothing can be added to it. An oak is never complete – it grows and changes throughout its life. The fallacy of completeness encourages learners to believe that if they ingest the textbook lesson-by-lesson, they will have swallowed the whole of the English language. Nothing could be further from the truth. Any course, any book, can only offer a sample of English. We can expect this sample to be interesting, and generative, in that it will encourage further language learning, but we cannot expect it to be a piece of the jigsaw, which, when fitted together, gives the whole language picture. The four levels of *Accelerate* are not intended to be done one after the other: they are suited to short course students at four different levels. They enable students to grow and develop at their own pace, acknowledging that learning English is something that continues and is not confined to the classroom.

We favour learning by doing. The approach in *Accelerate* is skills based, starting with language use about motivating topics. While each lesson focuses on language form appropriate to the level, that language form is there because the learners need it to carry out the activities and process the texts. Texts and activities are not devised in order to contextualize a pre-specified language syllabus. The language syllabus comes from the texts and activities themselves.

Using *Accelerate*

In creating these materials our aim has been to produce lessons that work: lessons that are transparent to the teacher and student. Each lesson takes a double-page spread, with a clear language focus and skills-summary box. Practice pages for each lesson give vital reinforcement of language focus points and help those learners who like to do extra work on their own. Flexibility is the keynote of *Accelerate*. The Student's Book provides the core, with its combination of lessons and practice pages; the Teacher's Book contains extra ideas for warmers and extension activities, enabling each teacher to tailor the materials to his or her class needs. The clarity and simplicity of the materials cuts teacher preparation time to a minimum and enables the teacher to concentrate on what he or she is best at – relating to and interacting with the students.

For some groups and teachers it will be appropriate to work through the lesson material step-by-step, and then look at the practice pages in class. For others, particularly mixed ability groups, the teacher may wish to refer to the Practice pages before, or during, an activity to clarify a language point. Where time is very short, Practice pages can be done out of class and the suggested homework omitted. Where there is more time, doing the Practice pages in class gives the teacher an opportunity to pay attention to individuals and do some remedial work. Most of the homework activities can also become classwork, if necessary, and we find that starting or ending a lesson by returning homework from a previous lesson is a valuable way of reviewing, particularly when students are able to read, compare and discuss each other's work. The homework is usually suitable for classroom display and will very quickly give an identity to the group and the room.

Most importantly *Accelerate* focuses on the learner: on his or her interests, experience, and ambitions. The great strength of starting from language skills rather than form is that the materials address the learner as a mature human-being. The learner is seen as someone with a lot to offer who may not speak a lot of English, rather than as someone to be addressed as if they were a child because they do not know much English. The word *accelerate* carries with it the idea of speed. These materials do not offer the possibility of covering the same familiar ground in some magically faster way. However they do enable learners to go faster by extending and revising their command of the language through activities that involve them as people.

Accelerate does not cover the whole of English grammar or the whole of the English language. What it does offer are a number of exciting windows into English, and opportunities for learners to climb through those windows and make English their own.

Map of the book

	Language focus	Skills focus
Unit 1 *Tradition*		
Lesson 1 Family celebrations Finding out about family celebrations in different countries	Prepositions of time Present simple	**Reading** for specific information **Speaking** and **writing**: interviewing
Lesson 2 Festivals Finding out about festivals in different countries	Present simple passive	**Reading** for specific information **Writing**: taking notes
Lesson 3 Customs Talking about customs in different countries	Present continuous Present continuous for the future	**Speaking**: discussing **Writing** an informal letter
Unit 2 *Sell it to me*		
Lesson 1 Where to go Planning a shopping trip	*Wh-* questions Countable and uncountable nouns	**Reading** and **listening** for specific information
Lesson 2 Mail order shopping Describing things to buy	Order of adjectives *Yes/No* questions	**Reading** for specific information **Speaking**: the *twenty questions* game
Lesson 3 Advertisements The language of advertisements	First conditional Comparative adjectives	**Listening** for detail **Writing** an advertisement
Unit 3 *Islands*		
Lesson 1 Which island? Describing an island and what it is like to live there	Superlative adjectives Definite and indefinite articles	**Reading** for main idea **Listening** for detail
Lesson 2 Survival at sea A true story about survival in the Pacific Ocean	Past simple Pronunciation of regular verbs in the past simple	**Reading**: ordering a text **Speaking**: speculating
Lesson 3 Skeleton Island Describing the features of an island	Prepositions of place Future with *going to*	**Speaking**: an information gap activity **Listening** for specific information
Unit 4 *Storytelling*		
Lesson 1 '... our dream's come true' Picture story: part 1	Present perfect simple *for* and *since*	**Reading** and **listening** for detail **Speaking**: roleplaying a conversation
Lesson 2 Cindy's crisis Picture story: part 2	*Should* for advice *have got to* for obligation	**Listening** for detail **Writing** an informal letter
Lesson 3 'I can't live without your love' Picture story: part 3	*will* for predictions Pronouns and possessive adjectives and pronouns	**Reading** and **listening** for detail **Writing** a song
Unit 5 *Family life*		
Lesson 1 What size family? Talking about large and small families	Zero conditional Talking about advantages and disadvantages	**Reading** a magazine article **Speaking**: discussing advantages and disadvantages
Lesson 2 House rules Childhood rules and punishments	*be allowed* and *could* for permission *have to* for obligation	**Speaking**: talking about family life **Listening** for specific information
Lesson 3 Family roles Comparing traditional family roles in different countries	Adverbs of frequency	**Speaking**: discussing family roles; interviewing **Listening** for specific information

	Language focus	Skills focus

Unit 6 *Time*

Lesson 1 Murder at Château Firenze A murder mystery story	Past continuous and past simple *anybody, nobody, somebody, everybody*	**Reading** and **listening** for specific information **Speaking**: speculating
Lesson 2 Time capsules Pyramids and other time capsules	Past simple passive Determiners: *some, a, an*	**Reading** and **listening** for specific information
Lesson 3 The Olympic Games Facts about the games and a general knowledge quiz	Direct and indirect *Wh-* questions	**Reading** and **listening** for specific information **Writing** questions

Unit 7 *Collectors' items*

Lesson 1 An unusual collection A collection of objects from airplanes and talking about travel experiences	Present perfect and past simple *already, yet* and *just*	**Speaking**: talking about collections and travel experiences **Listening** for specific information
Lesson 2 Collecting information Finding out about market research and conducting a class survey	Present perfect simple and present perfect continuous Polite requests	**Listening** for main idea **Writing**: conducting a survey and writing up notes
Lesson 3 'The Collector' Reading an extract from a novel	*-ing* form	**Reading** a narrative **Speaking**: roleplaying a police interview

Unit 8 *A week of entertainment*

Lesson 1 What's on? Choosing what to go to at a festival	Making and replying to suggestions Stating preferences	**Reading** for specific information **Speaking**: making arrangements
Lesson 2 A celebrity guest An explorer's adventures	Non-defining relative clauses Phrasal verbs	**Listening** for main ideas and detail **Writing** a publicity article
Lesson 3 Choosing a programme Designing a festival programme and brochure	Talking about likes and dislikes Expressing agreement and disagreement	**Speaking**: roleplaying a committee meeting **Writing**: making a festival programme

Unit 9 *The natural world*

Lesson 1 Whales Finding out about whales	Comparatives with *'as...as'* Revision of comparatives and superlatives Revision of present perfect	**Reading** a factual text for main idea and detail **Listening** to a radio discussion and expressing opinions
Lesson 2 Favourite animals Unusual pets and famous animals	Reported speech *say* and *tell*	**Listening** to and **writing** descriptions of animals **Reading** a newspaper article
Lesson 3 Nature at work Talking about climate and holidays	Short forms Past continuous	**Reading** and **writing** postcards **Listening** for main ideas and detail

Unit 10 *Into the unknown*

Lesson 1 The Blue Nile Two expeditions down the Nile	*too* and *enough* Past perfect	**Reading** for main ideas and detail **Speaking**: comparing information
Lesson 2 Cycling across the Andes A cycling expedition in South America	*have to* and *must* for obligation Revision of the *-ing* form	**Listening** and **reading** for main ideas and detail **Speaking**: planning an adventure trip
Lesson 3 Organising an expedition Planning an expedition and asking for sponsorship	Revision of future forms: Present continuous, *going to, will, hope to* and *hope (that)*	**Speaking**: discussing and organising an expedition **Writing** a formal letter

Unit 1 Tradition

This unit focuses on describing public festivals and family celebrations, and gives examples of how polite customs vary in different cultures around the world.

Lesson 1 *Family celebrations*

Aim: To focus on prepositions of time *in/on/at* and the use of the present continuous to describe what is happening in a photograph. (The use of the present continuous for future social arrangements is highlighted in Unit 1 Lesson 3.)

Language focus

1 Prepositions of time
on the wedding day
at lunch-time
in the afternoon

2 Present simple
The bride dresses in traditional Thai costume.
The bridegroom usually wears a suit.

Skills focus

- **Listening:** for information about a celebration
- **Reading:** a description for detail
- **Writing:** notes to prepare for writing a paragraph

Vocabulary focus

- Family celebrations
- Weddings: *bride, bridegroom, ceremony, diamond ring, presents, dress, priest, church, costume*

Warmer

To prepare for the topic of this lesson, find out whether any of the students has recently had, or is about to have a birthday, or any other family celebration. If so, let them tell the class very briefly how they celebrate, eg:
We always go to the restaurant on my birthday.
Everyone goes to my grandmother's house for New Year.
If no one has anything suitable to tell the class about, or if they do not feel confident at this stage, tell them briefly about how you celebrate, eg, your birthday.

1

Students should work either on their own or in pairs to look at the photographs and jot down their ideas. Let them do this quickly.
The students should then work in pairs to exchange their ideas. Finally let some pairs tell the class what they think is happening. Put the ideas on the board.
▣ Now the students listen to the cassette and note down which picture is being described. If necessary, play the cassette a second time for students to note any key words which helped them decide, and to write down the name of the celebration.
Students work in pairs to discuss similar festivals in their culture. Let some different pairs report back to the class.

Answers
Brigitte is talking about the photograph on the right.
The name of the festival is Kermes.

2

Introduce the theme of weddings. You might like to show some photos of a wedding, or ask if anyone in the class has been to one recently. Do not spend long on this, though, as students discuss weddings in Activity 5.
The students now work in pairs to match the words and pictures. (The vocabulary will help them with the reading in Activity 3.) Tell them to try to guess any words they do not know.
Check the answers round the class.

Answers
2 – *d*   3 – *g*   4 – *h*   5 – *c*   6 – *e*   7 – *j*   8 – *i*   9 – *b*   10 – *a*
Students now work in small groups to say what they think happens at a Thai wedding. Ask the students to cover the reading passage on the next page, so they do not cheat! You may need to explain that *Thai* is the adjective connected with *Thailand*, and check that students know where Thailand is.
The groups should note down their main ideas, and then, in turn, report back to the class.
You may want to go through Language Summary 2 on practice page 66 either now or after Activity 3.

3

The students should read this passage to themselves. They should find most of the unfamiliar vocabulary has been explained in the previous activity.
After they have been through the passage, let them discuss it briefly in pairs or small groups, and check which of their ideas were correct.
You could do practice page 66 Exercise 2 now.

UNIT 1 LESSON 1

4

Students work on their own to answer the comprehension questions. Check that they are all familiar with *wh-* questions, and if there are any problems, do some remedial work on them afterwards.
Check the answers round the class.

Answers
1 *The bride wears traditional Thai costume and the bridegroom wears a western-style suit.*
2 *The monks come to the bride's house and bless the offerings.*
3 *At a hotel.*
4 *The most important person at the wedding (usually the oldest member of the family).*
5 *For luck.*
6 *Thai or Chinese food.*
7 *Household goods or money.*
8 *No.*

5

Students work on their own to prepare their lists, and then work in pairs on the questions and answers. Encourage them to use *wh-* questions, and go round monitoring and helping as necessary. You may need to brainstorm some ideas on the board first. If the class is the same nationality, brainstorm the different traditions that occur in different regions of their country.

6

If your class is multilingual, you could organize the students into groups with different nationalities to compare traditions. In any case, encourage them to appoint a secretary to make notes so that they can report back to the class.

Homework

Students may like to use their notes from Activities 5 and 6 as preparation for the written homework. Or they can talk about any other celebration – their notes from Activity 1 could also be useful.
If you have a keen class, encourage them to present their work in an attractive way with pictures for a classroom display.

Practice *page 66*

1

You will probably find it a good idea to go through Language Summary 1 to check that students understand the use of these three time prepositions.
They should complete the expressions on their own.
Go through the answers with the class.

Answers
1 *in* 2 *at* 3 *at* 4 *on* 5 *on* 6 *in* 7 *in* 8 *in* 9 *at* 10 *at*
11 *at* 12 *on* 13 *in* 14 *in* 15 *in*

2

Refer students back to Lesson 1 Activities 3 and 4. You may need to draw their attention to Language Summary 2 for the negative form.
They should do the exercise working on their own or in pairs.
Check the answers round the class.

Answers
2 *takes place*   3 *gives*   4 *celebrates*
5 *in*   6 *is*   7 *in*
8 *on*   9 *in*   10 *is*
11 *in*   12 *is*   13 *come*
14 *have*   15 *travel*   16 *At*
17 *don't have*   18 *have*   19 *in*
20 *at*   21 *eat*   22 *eats*
23 *are*   24 *is*   25 *play*
26 *talk*   27 *At*   28 *go*
29 *watch*   30 *don't have* 31 *eat*
32 *drink*

3

This exercise practises some of the words from the lesson. Let students work in pairs or small groups. You could have a competition to see which group finishes first and gets all the answers right. Give a point for each correct answer, an additional point for correct pronunciation, and, if you like, one or two more points for the words used correctly in a sentence.
You can always use this technique to practise spellings. The students may like to make up their own anagrams and then exchange them with a partner to solve them.

Answers
1 RING 2 FLOWERS 3 BRIDE 4 WEDDING 5 PRESENTS
6 CEREMONY

UNIT 1 LESSON 2

Lesson 2 *Festivals*

Aims: To learn about some public festivals from other countries and to use the present simple in descriptions.

Language focus

Present simple passive
Money is collected.
The ship is burnt at sea.

Skills focus

- **Reading:** three passages for detail
- **Writing:** taking notes while reading
- **Listening:** for information about a festival

Vocabulary focus

- Festivals: *custom, procession, to take place, to participate, to celebrate, public*

Review

If students have presented their homework paragraphs with illustrations, display them around the class. Let the students read each other's work, talk to or question the author of one piece, and perhaps have a short class discussion on the paragraph they found most interesting.

Warmer

Tell the students that they are now going to learn about some public festivals. (The one most focused on in the last lesson, marriage, is a private or family festival.) Give them a few minutes to think of any festivals they know of, either from their own country, or others. Make a note of them on the board.

1

The students now work in pairs to answer the questions. Tell them to cover the reading passages and to make guesses. Remind them to speculate on the time of year and the reason for the festival. For example, eggs may remind them of spring, perhaps of Easter; fires are often associated with autumn or winter.
Let a few pairs report their ideas to the class, and see if there is general agreement.

2

Britain has hundreds of unique regional festivals occurring at various times of the year. Some festivals only take place in one particular town and many have ancient historical origins.
You can highlight the use of the present simple passive in the descriptions:
A: are eaten; is shown
B: is collected; are chased
C: is carried; is followed; is burnt
You may wish to go through the Language Summary from practice page 67 now, and get the students to do Exercise 1. Tell the students that they should not worry if there are words in the passage that they do not know. At this stage they are just looking for clues to match the passages and photos. They should work either on their own or in pairs.
Let a few pairs report back to the class. Encourage them to give reasons, for example:
I think passage C goes with picture 1 because of the fire.

Answers
Picture 1: Up-Helly-Aa
Picture 2: Minehead Hobby Horse
Picture 3: Egg-rolling

3

Encourage the students to guess the meanings of the vocabulary using the context, ie they should refer to the passages. Again, they should work either on their own or in pairs. Check the answers with the class.

Answers
A: 1b 2d 3a 4c
B: 1c 2a 3d 4b
C: 1b 2c 3d 4a

4

The *wh-* word prompts focus the students on the important information in the text. Remind the class that notes cover essential information only, and that they do not need to write full sentences. They should certainly not copy the full sentences from the texts.
While they are working on their own or in pairs to complete the table, draw up a blank table on the board. Then call on different students to fill in the different boxes with their answers. Encourage members of the class to make any necessary corrections.

UNIT 1 LESSON 2

Answers

	Minehead hobby horse	Up-Helly-Aa
where it takes place	Minehead, SW England	Shetland Isles, Scotland
when it takes place	1 May	31 January
who participates	a man dressed as a horse, children	festival chief, 40 other men
why there is a festival	brings luck on May Day	end of Holy Days
what happens	horse walks through town, bows to sun, visits local castle and 2 towns, dances in square, chases children, collects money	model of Viking ship carried through streets, procession with torches, ship is burnt, parties until morning

5

 First let the students look at the photo and speculate briefly about what kind of festival is involved. Then, for the first listening, write the two gist questions on the board and ask the students to close their books.

Answers
The festival takes place on the island of Bali, in Indonesia. It celebrates the birthday of the village temple or church.

 Tell the students to copy down the headings from Activity 4 and try to fill in the information from what they remember on the first listening. Then play the cassette again. Play it a third time to check if necessary.

Answers

name	Odalan
where it takes place	Bali, Indonesia
when it takes place	once every Balinese year, usually every 210 days
who participates	adults and children
why there is a festival	to celebrate the birthday of the village temple
what happens	women take offerings to the temple, prayers and music, dancing at the temple in the evening, procession on last day

6

You may want to brainstorm festivals and write them on the board, or to refer to the list of festivals the students thought of at the beginning of this lesson.
Remind the students to write in note form, but to use full sentences when they are telling the rest of their group about the festival. If you have a multilingual class, you may wish to make up groups of different nationalities so that they can tell each other something new and interesting.
Go round monitoring and helping as necessary. Remind the students that this is useful preparation for their homework.

Homework

The students can use their notes from Activity 6. Remind them that they have to write in full sentences. They should try to make their descriptions clear and simple.

Practice *page 67*

1

Go through the Language Summary with the class, if necessary. Remind them that it is not always necessary to have an agent.
They should do the exercise on their own, then mark each other's work in pairs.

Answers
2 *are grown*   3 *are picked*   4 *are taken*
5 *are pressed*   6 *is poured*   7 *is added*
8 *is left*   9 *is bottled*   10 *are sold*
11 *are distributed*   12 *is drunk*

If a number of students have difficulties with the irregular past participles, you may need to do some remedial work.

2

This is a simple transformation exercise, which also gives further practice with *wh-* questions. Students can do the exercise and check it in the same way as the previous one.

Answers
2 *Where are the grapes grown?*
3 *When are the grapes picked?*
4 *Where are the grapes taken (to)?*
5 *What are the grapes pressed by?*
6 *What is the juice poured into?*
7 *What is added to help fermentation?*
8 *How long is the wine left (for)?*
9 *When is the wine bottled?*
10 *Who are the bottles sold to?/To whom are the bottles sold?*
11 *Where are the cases of wine distributed to?*
12 *Where is the final product drunk?*

3

This is another fun activity to practise new words, which can also be done as a team game. Give two points to the first team to finish, one to the second, and take one point from the last team. Then give one point for each correct answer, and one for each word correctly pronounced (as single words, not as joined words). Take points off for wrong answers and incorrect pronunciation.

Answers
2 *FESTIVAL ALWAYS*   3 *LIFE FEMALE*   4 *CASTLE LETTER*
5 *COSTUME MEN*   6 *TORCH CHURCH*

UNIT 1 LESSON 3

Lesson 3 *Customs*

Aims: To learn about polite customs in different parts of the world and to practise the conventions of informal letters, including contractions, punctuation and expressions used in informal letters.

Language focus

1 Contractions, used in informal letters
I'm so pleased that you're visiting us.

2 Present continuous
He's dipping his food in his coffee.
She's eating with her fingers.

3 Present continuous for future social arrangements
My sister's getting married on the 30th.

Skills focus

- **Reading:** a letter for detail
- **Writing:** an informal letter
- **Listening:** for information about polite customs

Vocabulary focus

- National Customs: *rude, polite, gesture, visitor, local, penfriend, informal*

Review

Students give their homework paragraphs to a partner to read. They then tell each other what they can remember about the festival. Some students can tell the class. They can also look out for errors in each other's work, but encourage them to do this sensitively. Deal with any general problems of language that arise, especially problems with prepositions of time, and present simple.

Warmer

If you feel it is right for your class, act out some deliberately rude situations, such as yawning without excusing yourself, etc. and note the students' reactions. You could then comment, eg:
Teachers are not usually rude to their students.
Polite people do not yawn in public.
Get the students to suggest one or two other similar social conventions.
This both draws students' attention to the topic of the lesson, and reminds them of the present simple.

1

Students should work in pairs or small groups to discuss pictures 1 to 4. Some suggestions should be reported back to the class and noted on the board.
As they speculate on what is happening in the pictures, they should also try to guess in which countries they are set.
▶ The class now listen to the cassette to find the two sets of answers. You may need to play the cassette twice.

Answers
India – picture 4   Japan – picture 1   Thailand – picture 3
Picture 1 – sneezing in public
Picture 2 – putting one's chopsticks into the bowl of rice that everyone is using
Picture 3 – pointing one's feet at someone
Picture 4 – eating with one's left hand

2

The students continue working in pairs to discuss the pictures and what is happening in them. As they do so, they may also discuss whether this behaviour causes offence in their own country or countries. The marks they make should, however, reflect their own feelings, and their ideas may lead to discussion, especially in a multilingual class where groups include different nationalities.
They then match the pictures with the captions.

Answers
  a – 3   b – 6   c – 5   d – 2   e – 4   f – 1
If your students have problems with the present continuous, refer to Language Summary 1 on practice page 68, and let them do Exercises 1 and 2.

3

In a multilingual class this activity should provide plenty of cultural comparisons. Organize the class into groups to distribute the nationalities. In a monolingual class the students may have different opinions about what is rude or polite.

4

Ask around the class if anyone has a penfriend. Have they met their penfriend, either in their own country, or by visiting the penfriend? Point out that this is an informal letter between friends.
Draw the students' attention to the form of the verbs – present continuous with future meaning. You could go through Language Summary 2 on practice page 68, and then tell the class to complete Exercises 3 and 4.

Answers
Kate tells Yoshi to bring something smart to wear to the wedding, a wedding present (not too expensive) and an umbrella.

Homework

Students can use their work on describing a public festival or family celebration from Lessons 1 and 2 for ideas to include in their letter, as well as any notes they made in Activity 3. They should use the letter in Activity 4 as a model.

Practice *page 68*

1

Refer students back to Lesson 3 Activities 1 and 2.
This construction should give students no problems, but you may need to remind them of spelling changes, eg *take – taking, sit – sitting*.
Let the students discuss the picture in pairs or small groups before they write their sentences. Check the answers with the class.

Answers
2 *The girl is drinking some wine.*
3 *The grandmother is passing the bread to the mother.*
4 *The mother is taking some/a slice of bread.*
5 *The young man is feeding the baby.*
6 *The dog is taking some/a piece of chicken from a plate.*

2

Either do this exercise orally with the whole class, or let the students work in pairs to ask and answer questions about the picture before they write their answers. Make sure they get the correct word order, and give extra drilling if there are any general problems. Check the answers with the class.

Answers
2 *Yes, they are.*
3 *The parents aren't drinking.*
4 *No, she isn't (sitting down).*
5 *The baby is eating.*
6 *No, he isn't (eating). (He's feeding the baby.)*

3

Refer students back to Lesson 3 Activity 4.
This exercise also gives practice with time prepositions. The students should work on their own to write Kate's arrangements, and then exchange work with a partner to mark each other's exercises. Go round monitoring and explain or drill any general problems.

Answers
2 *On Tuesday afternoon she's playing tennis with Sara./On Tuesday she's playing tennis with Sara in the afternoon.*
3 *On Wednesday at 10am she's going to the dentist.*
4 *On Thursday at 7.30pm she's having dinner with Sam.*
5 *On Friday evening she's meeting Tom at the disco.*
6 *On Saturday at 9am she's working at Dino's.*
7 *On Sunday at 3pm she's taking Yoshi to the airport.*

4

If necessary tell the class one or two of your plans for next week, and then get some students to tell the class what they are doing. They then each write five diary entries, for different days.
Go round monitoring and helping while students ask their partners about their arrangements.

Unit 2 Sell it to me

This unit concerns different aspects of the topic of shopping: where to go, types of shops, describing things to buy, and advertisements and slogans.

Lesson 1 *Where to go*

Aims: To practise *wh-* questions with *wh-* as the subject and the object and to learn about where to go shopping and different types of shops.

Language focus

1 *wh-* questions
Where can you buy travel and guide books?
Which shop sells ballet videos?

2 Countable and uncountable nouns
How many shops are open on Sunday?
How much money can you save at The Italian Connection?

Skills focus

- **Reading:** scanning a shopping guide for information
- **Listening:** to conversations for information
- **Speaking:** making and explaining choices

Vocabulary focus

- Leisure activities: *guide, museum, theatre, restaurant, bar, cuisine, craft fair*
- Shops and shopping: *bookshop, market, stall, antiques*

Review

Take in the homework letters. If there are any general problems with prepositions of time or use of the present continuous with future meaning, do some extra work on these topics.

Warmer

Explain to the class that Covent Garden is a large shopping area in central London. It used to be a covered fruit and vegetable market (ie a market with a roof over it) but the whole area was renovated as a shopping and entertainment area, with a wide variety of shops, some of which are quite expensive. Covent Garden is very popular with Londoners and tourists, and is usually very busy. There are plenty of places here to eat and drink, and it is not far from the main London theatres. Performers and musicians come to Covent Garden to perform, play and sing, entertain the public and make some money. When they have finished, they pass round a hat for the public to put money in.
Ask the students if they have ever visited anywhere like this.

1

The class should work in pairs or small groups for a short time to talk about the photograph.

Answer

The photograph shows some street theatre, with someone juggling and a large crowd watching. The place is Covent Garden.

2

The text for the scan reading activity is an authentic shopping guide to Covent Garden. You should set a time limit for this activity. Remind students that they do not need to read and understand every word, but that they should look for key words in the text to help them answer the questions. They should work on their own, or, if necessary, in pairs.
Students should be familiar with *wh-* questions which follow the order:
Q word + auxiliary + subject + main verb (+ direct object)?
Where   can   you   buy   travel and guide books?

If they have problems, go through Language Summary 1 on practice page 69, and let the class do Exercise 1.

Answers

2 *Trouts*
3 *The shops in Covent Garden Market; Dillons Arts Bookshop*
4 *071 379 6344*
5 *Monkey Business*
6 *£2*
7 *Dillons Arts Bookshop*
8 *Ponti's of Covent Garden*
9 *over 50*
10 *Saturday and Sunday*
11 *The Italian Connection*
12 *24 hours a day*
13 *8 hours*
14 *Royal Opera House Shop*
15 *Jubilee Market Hall (on Mondays) and Covent Garden Market*

You could do practice page 69 Exercise 2 here.

3

Tell the students to listen to the background noise during the conversations, as this provides additional clues to the setting. They should also listen for key words, such as *novel, stories, books* in part 1, *pizza, pasta, lasagne* in part 2, *train, Piccadilly line, platform* in part 3, and *maps, South America, mountains* in part 4. You will need to play the cassette at least twice.
If the class have had difficulty with this activity, play the cassette again, pausing after the answers or key words.

Answers

1 *Dillons Arts Bookshop*
2 *The Italian Connection*
3 *London Transport information*
4 *Stanfords*

UNIT 2 LESSON 1

4

This activity gives practice in making suggestions and giving reasons for choices of places to visit. Make sure the groups keep their suggestions simple. If necessary, brainstorm a few reasons on the board first. You could encourage students to react to suggestions with such comments as:
We like fish and chips too.
Oh, do you? We prefer pizza.

5

Make sure the students understand that they should write their questions on their own, but work in groups to get answers. This activity is useful preparation for the homework.

Homework

This could be done in groups. Research into local shops is a good idea, and may involve visiting the shops or looking in the telephone directory and calling them. The activity could be done in class time as a mini-project. Students should look out for any free brochures or advertising materials, including, for example, paper bags with shops' names on, or local postcards, to illustrate their guides. The students' guides could then be put on the classroom wall for everyone to read.

Practice *page 69*

Language Summary 1

Refer the students to Lesson 1 Activity 2. They should not have any difficulty with these questions. If there do seem to be problems, put a list of all the *wh-* question words on the board.

1

Students should complete the sentences on their own. Go round the class to check the answers.

Answers
2 *What size is this T-shirt?*
3 *Where can I find the nearest bookshop?*
4 *Who is going to the museum?*
5 *Why do you want a map of Africa?*
6 *Whose is this poster? Whose poster is this?*
7 *Which pizza would you like?*
8 *Who wants an ice cream?*

2

Go through the first two examples with the class. Make sure they all understand that *who* refers to people, and may be used as an object. (*Whom did you meet at the theatre?* sounds very formal to an English person.) *What* refers to things.
Let students complete the exercise on their own and check their answers in pairs.

Answers
3 *Who gave you a free ticket?*
4 *What ballet did you see at Covent Garden?*
5 *What happened during the performance?*
6 *What did they find?*

3

Make sure the class understand the difference between *How much?* and *How many?* You could extend the activity by telling them each to think of six to ten further items to give to their partner to group correctly.

Answers

countable	uncountable
hours	food
maps	information
museums	pasta
theatres	wine
videos	

4

Let students work in pairs to ask and answer the questions before they write them down. Check the answers round the class. You may find it useful to list different quantity words on the board first, eg, *slice (of bread, cake), bar (of soap, chocolate), box, packet, can, bottle, jar (of jam), tin, bag.*

Answers
3 *How much pizza would you like? Two slices, please.*
4 *How many pens would you like? One blue one, please.*
5 *How much rice would you like? One packet, please.*
6 *How many cans of lemonade would you like? One can, please.*
7 *How many bars of chocolate would you like? Two bars, please.*
8 *How many sweets would you like? Six, please.*

UNIT 2 LESSON 2

Lesson 2 *Mail order shopping*

Aims: To give practice with different types of *yes/no* questions and to introduce students to the order of adjectives in describing things. The topic is shopping by post from a catalogue which has a photograph and description of each item.

Language focus

1 *Yes/no* questions
Is it made of plastic?
Do you use it in the bathroom?

2 Order of adjectives
a large red Indian silk and cotton waistcoat
a pocket-sized black Japanese plastic calculator

Skills focus

- **Reading:** a catalogue for information
- **Writing:** a description of an article for a catalogue
- **Listening**: to a game and then playing it
- **Speaking:** playing a game

Vocabulary focus

- Describing objects
- Adjectives of size: *small, medium, large*
- Colours
- Materials: *silk, cotton, leather, plastic*

Review

Display the shopping guides around the room and make sure everyone has a chance to study them. Then let each student decide on two places they would like to visit, with a reason. They exchange ideas with a partner or in small groups.

Warmer

Try and get hold of some mail order catalogues to bring in and show the class. If you have enough, or do not mind cutting one up, let everyone in the class, working in groups, choose one item to buy for themselves and one to buy for someone else. They may give reasons for their choices, which do not have to be serious.
If you cannot bring in such catalogues, find out whether anyone in the class has shopped by mail order, and, if so, whether they found it satisfactory.

1

The students should work in pairs to match the descriptions and pictures. It does not matter if they do not understand all the words in the descriptions.

Answers
2 – c   3 – e   4 – a   5 – d   6 – b

Now explain or get the students to guess any new vocabulary, for example *multicoloured, canvas*.
Each student then chooses two items, one to buy for themselves, and one for someone else. They exchange ideas with a partner, and give reasons for their choices.

2

If necessary check names of the countries and nationality adjectives, ie *India/Indian, Japan/Japanese, Africa/African, China/Chinese, Italy/Italian, Canada/Canadian*. You could point out the countries on a world map if you have one in the classroom, and ask the students if they own anything made in another country.
The students work alone or in pairs to complete the table. Point out that adjectives in English follow this order when there are several of them before a noun.
You may want to go through Language Summary 1 on practice page 70 here. The students could then do Exercise 2.

Answers

size	colour	origin	material	noun
large	red	Indian	silk and cotton	waistcoat
pocket-sized	black	Japanese	plastic	calculator
–	multi-coloured	African	glass	jewellery
50cm high	blue and white	Chinese	ceramic	vase
small/ medium/large	brown or black	Italian	leather	belt
medium and large	green and brown	Canadian	canvas and leather	suitcases

3

If necessary, check that the students know what each of these items is (teapot, chess set, pocket watch). They should not need any new adjectives, but should choose from those in Activities 1 and 2. They may find it helpful to set out the adjectives in table form first, to get the right order. Draw their attention to the fact that in the catalogue descriptions the information is broken up into small chunks, and that only some of the adjectives appear with the noun on the first line of the description. The price is usually given last. Sometimes the country of origin appears as an adjective, and sometimes in the form *made in* or *from* with the name of the country.

The class will probably find it easier to do this activity in pairs or small groups. Go round monitoring and giving help where needed. This activity is useful preparation for the homework. It would be good to do Exercise 3 on practice page 70 here. As a follow-up to this, get students to write a description of a favourite possession. They should do this on their own, and then tell their partner about the item and why it is important to them. Let some pairs report to the class about their partner's possession.

4

This is a common game in Britain called 'Twenty Questions'. It was a popular radio game, and is still played as a quiz game. Explain that all the questions must be answered by *yes* or *no*. Tell the students to try to guess the item as they listen. They should write their guesses down, not call them out. Pause the cassette just before Luke says 'Um, the stereo system?' and ask the students if they have guessed what the object is.
This would be a good place to go through Language Summary 2 on practice page 70, and for the students to do Exercise 4. The game could be played in two teams in class. Ensure the students use a variety of *yes/no* question forms, eg *Is it ... Can you ... Does it ...?*

Homework

The descriptions do not need to be very long. You may like to brainstorm some items in class and put a list of useful adjectives on the board.

Practice *page 70*

1

This is a fun activity to practise some of the new vocabulary. All the words read left to right or top to bottom in the square. You could make this a competition, either for individuals, or for pairs or groups. As with previous games, give points to the first teams to finish, and deduct from the last. Then give or deduct points for correct or incorrect pronunciation. You could give extra points for words correctly used in sentences.

Answers

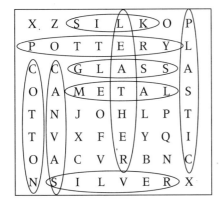

2

The order of adjectives in Language Summary 1 is the same as in the table in Lesson 2 Activity 2. Point out that if the origin is expressed in the form *from Africa* or *made in Japan*, this information also goes after the noun. The comma after the size adjective is optional.
The students should work on their own to complete the exercise, and then exchange their work with a partner to check it.

Answers
2 *A long, blue Indian shirt.*
3 *A small, green Italian car with a sunroof.*
4 *A large, red and gold Chinese calendar.*
5 *A black American steel tennis racquet.*
6 *An Italian leather handbag with a shoulder strap.*
7 *A small Japanese computer with a laser printer.*
8 *A pair of small Swiss sunglasses.*

3

Students should work on their own. Then let them tell their partner about their items. Some students can report back to the class. Remind them to try to vary their descriptions by putting some of the information after the noun.

Language Summary 2

This should be a reminder for the students of something they already know. If there are general problems, give them several statements with both full and auxiliary verbs, and do transformation drills with the class.

4

Refer the class back to Lesson 2 Activity 4.
The students should write the questions on their own, and then ask and answer them with a partner, to give additional oral practice.

Answers
2 *Is it made of glass?*
3 *Can anyone use it?*
4 *Is it round?*
5 *Is it square?*
6 *Is it mechanical?*
7 *Does it make a noise?*
8 *Can you use it outside?*
9 *Can you use it anytime?*
10 *Is it usually used in the bathroom?*
   The object is a mirror.

UNIT 2 LESSON 3

Lesson 3 *Advertisements*

Aims: To give practice with comparative forms of adjectives and their spelling rules, and to prepare a radio advertisement. The topic is advertising – magazine adverts and product slogans, and radio adverts.

Language focus

1 First conditional
If you eat Garden Farm low fat margarine, you will be healthier.
You will be healthier if you eat Garden Farm low fat margarine.

2 Comparison of adjectives: comparatives
Get a bigger bar!
The more reliable way to be on time every day!

Skills focus

- **Listening:** to an advertisement for detail
- **Reading:** and matching slogans and products
- **Writing:** a radio advertisement

Vocabulary focus

- Comparative adjectives: *cleaner, bigger, tastier, wider, better, more interesting*
- Everyday objects: *alarm clock, deodorant, margarine, washing powder*
- Sports: *squash, tennis, badminton, football, scuba diving, rock climbing*

Review

Play a game of Twenty Questions with the class. Make sure they vary their *yes/no* questions. Students could use the items they described for homework. Or, students could work in small groups to guess each other's items. Demonstrate with the whole class first: the student says, eg, *It's long, blue, and made of silk.* (A silk dress.) The rest of the group then try to guess the item. You may like to limit the number of questions they can ask, eg, to five. They can ask direct questions, such as *Is it a silk dress?* or indirect ones, such as *Is it clothing?*

Warmer

It would be useful to bring in some well-known and some less well-known advertisements from magazines, with the product names removed or covered (these can be in your local language – whatever the students are most likely recognize) and ask the students if they know what is being advertised. Or you could say (or sing) one or two advertising slogans.

1

The adverts chosen are deliberately ambiguous and should provoke discussion and speculation. Students should justify their choice of product for each advert, saying, eg, *I think it's an aquarium because...* Some pairs should report back to the class.

Answers
1 – *b*   2 – *c*   3 – *b*

2

If students are having problems with this, check that they understand all the words in the left-hand column. Note that washing up liquid is for washing dishes, while washing powder is for washing clothes. Let the students work in pairs, and check the answers round the class.

Answers
2 – *d*   3 – *a*   4 – *f*   5 – *g*   6 – *c*   7 – *b*

Ask students which words helped them to decide on a match for each product and slogan, for example, *margarine* and *butter* are used on bread or for cooking; *deodorant* is to *dry* perspiration; *chocolate* is sold in *bars*; *washing up liquid* is used for washing *dishes* by *hand*; a *language centre* is a place for *learning* languages, like *English*; *washing powder* makes *clothes clean*; an *alarm clock* wakes you up, and helps you be *on time*.

3

This exercise gives practice with the comparative form of adjectives, as well as with the first conditional. You could refer to Language Summaries 1 and 2 on practice page 71, and ask the students to do Exercise 1. Let the students work alone to complete the sentences, and then compare answers in pairs.

Suggested answers
2 *If you use this deodorant, you will stay drier all day.*
3 *You get a bigger bar if you buy this chocolate.*
4 *You will have softer hands if you wash your dishes with this liquid.*
5 *It is easier to learn English if you use this language centre.*
6 *If you use this washing powder, your clothes will be cleaner.*
7 *If you use this alarm clock, you will be on time every day.*

The students can work in pairs to think up product names. The pairs should then join with another pair to explain why they have chosen the name, eg, *Garden Farm margarine sounds natural and healthy.*
To extend the activity, each group can then report back one name per product to the class, and the whole class can vote on each name to have a class list of product names, again with reasons for the choices.

4

🔊 Make sure the students have studied the table and know what they are listening for. You will probably need to play the cassette two or three times. The first time the students should just listen. Let them see what they can remember before you play it the second time. If they are having problems, pause the cassette during each part for them to hear the answers.

UNIT 2 LESSON 3

Answers

Name of shop /company	What is being advertised	Selling points
2 Hobson's	bread and cakes	fresher than supermarket ones bigger selection tastier bread and cakes
3 Sunshine Company	Far East holidays	more exciting than Europe all popular locations cheaper prices than last year better choice of hotels 10% discount this month sunnier holidays

If you have not already looked at Language Summary 2 on practice page 71, this is a good place to do so. Students can do Exercise 3 now.

5

Working alone or in pairs, students should try to complete the sentences, using comparative adjectives from the table in Activity 4.
🔊 Now play the cassette for the class to check their answers. If there are any problems, play it a second time, pausing before the relevant words.

Answers
2 *bigger* 3 *wider* 4 *more exciting* 5 *sunnier*
6 *more enjoyable* 7 *better* 8 *cheaper*

6

You may want to brainstorm places or products and write them on the board. A list of persuasive comparative adjectives might also be useful. Remind the students that the advertisements need to be fairly short, but they should give good reasons for choosing the place or product, and include a comparison with a competitor, or show how the facilities or product have been improved. This activity is useful practice for the homework.

Homework

If possible, record all the class's radio adverts on a cassette. Get them to practise reading aloud first and help them by marking where to pause for breath in their text and what intonation to use, for example, 'Feel tired? Always got a headache?' both need a rising tone at the end because they are questions. Students could add background music to their recordings.
If a cassette recorder is not available, get the students to perform their advert in front of the class.

Practice *page 71*

Language Summary 1

Refer the class back to Lesson 3 Activity 3. Go through the structure pattern of the first conditional with them. If you think it is necessary, drill the structure.

1

The students should complete this exercise on their own. They can check their partner's answers, or you can check them round the class.

Answers
2 *will go, use* 3 *will have, brush* 4 *look, will see*
5 *will give, book* 6 *buy, will give*

2

In this exercise the students make up their own endings. They can work in pairs. Go round monitoring and correcting. Let two or three pairs tell the class their answer for each question. If there are general problems, you will need to do some remedial practice.

Language Summary 2

Highlight the spelling rules for comparative adjectives. If you feel it is useful, put several adjectives of each type on the board and ask different students to give you the comparative form, and then see if they can tell you the rule for forming that comparative. You could make this into a team competition, with the class divided into two teams.

3

Students complete the exercise on their own, checking their answers with a partner.

Answers
2 *Melons are more expensive than pears.*
3 *A holiday in Greece is cheaper than a holiday in Switzerland.*
4 *Glass is heavier than plastic.*
5 *Planes are quicker than trains.*
6 *You can buy more unusual things in a market than in a shopping centre.*
7 *Supermarkets are more convenient than small shops.*
8 *Fruit is better for you than chocolate.*

4

You can make this a team competition, giving points in the usual way. Note that when we say these compound nouns, we put the main stress on the first word.

Answers
alarm *clock*, **leis**ure *park*, **trav**el *agents*, **hair***dresser*, **wild***life park*

13

Unit 3 Islands

This unit is based on the topic of islands: vocabulary and description of location and features, listening to the problems of living on a remote island, a survival story (describing feelings) and information gap and problem-solving speaking activities.

Lesson 1 Which island?

Aims: to practise the superlative forms of adjectives and use of the article; to describe islands around the world and to listen to the problems of living on a remote island.

Language focus

1 Comparison of adjectives – superlatives
Santa Cruz is the second largest island in the Galapagos.
It is one of the most expensive places in the world.

2 Articles – definite and indefinite
The Galapagos are an isolated groups of islands on the equator.
A Bishop from Panama discovered the Galapagos in 1535.

Skills focus

- **Reading:** a passage for information
- **Listening:** to a description for detail
- **Writing:** notes on a spoken description and writing a new description

Vocabulary focus

- Places: *island, islet, mainland, national park*
- Geographical location: *compass points, north of ..., northern, south east of ...*
- Occupations: *bishop, sailor, pirate, hunter, tourist*
- Industries: *tourism, fishing, farming*
- Miscellaneous: *inhabited, isolated, population*

Review

To recycle material from the previous lesson, collect authentic adverts from a magazine, ask the students to choose three that they like, and get them to write a conditional sentence for each advert. Students compare in groups what they wrote.

Warmer

Tell the class that the topic of this lesson is islands, and brainstorm islands that they know, either in English, or in their own language. You could make it into a competition, dividing the class into groups and giving them a few minutes to write down all the islands they know. Give one point for each island, two if the group know the correct English name, and three if no other group has thought of that island.

1

This activity requires some geographical knowledge so most of the island shapes chosen are well known, eg, Britain, Japan. Iceland and the Galapagos may be more difficult. You could point out the islands on a world map if you have one in class. The students can work in pairs to discuss the names.

Answers
1 *The Galapagos* 2 *Iceland* 4 *New Zealand*
5 *Crete* 6 *Japan*

Write up the names of continents (Europe, Asia, etc) and points of the compass on the board if your students are unsure of this to help them answer the next question. They can continue to work in pairs.

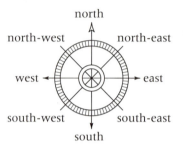

Answers
2 *Crete* 3 *Iceland* 4 *Japan* 5 *Britain* 6 *New Zealand*

2

The students should work on their own to scan the text for the answers. Remind them that they do not need to understand all the words. Get them to justify their answers to the true/false statements by indicating the words in the text that helped them.

Answers
1 true (in 1535)
2 false (The Bishop named the islands)
3 true
4 false (1,000 km west of Ecuador)
5 true (volcanic islands)
6 true (Five of the islands are inhabited)
7 false (It is one of the most expensive places in the world to visit)

3

The students continue to work on their own. Now they have to skim the paragraphs for gist.

Answers
early history – 2
geography and population – 1
why the islands are famous – 4
industries – 1
how the islands got their name – 2
recent history – 3

UNIT 3 LESSON 1

4

Tell the class to re-read the passage about the Galapagos Islands to try to get an idea of what life there might be like. Put some suggestions on the board. The words they will hear will probably reflect the way of life on the islands.

On the first listening students check their vocabulary predictions.

Answers

You hear the words *cities, nature, fresh water, coffee, electricity, generator, radio station, cinema, bus, education.*

5

Tell the students to work in pairs to note down any advantages and disadvantages of living on the islands they can remember. They then listen to the cassette and note down any they did not have. It might be easier if one partner noted down advantages and the other disadvantages.

You may need to play the cassette a third time to check students have got all the points.

Answers

Advantages: the simplicity of life, contact with nature, solitude, freedom

Disadvantages: not enough fresh water, electricity limited, no TV, one radio station, one cinema with old films, one bus, no high school

6

You may like to get some suggestions to put on the board, and brainstorm advantages and disadvantages. For younger students, this could be done in pairs or small groups. The students could produce their work in the form of a poster with photographs and drawings to put on the wall.

Homework

Language Summary 1 on practice page 72 gives information about superlative adjectives, and Exercise 1 would be useful practice for the homework.

Practice *page 72*

Language Summary 1

If necessary, go through Language Summary 1 with the class before they do Exercise 1. Remind students that the comparative is used with two items, and is often used with *than*, while the superlative is used for three or more items, or used 'absolutely', often with phrases like *in the world*, or the present perfect and *ever*, as in *the best I have ever seen.*

1

Students should work on their own, or you may like to do the exercise orally with the whole class.

Answers

3 *the best* 4 *sunnier* 5 *the wettest* 6 *heavier*
7 *the most interesting* 8 *more exciting*

Language Summary 2

Note also that *a* is used for new information, and *the* is used for something we already know:

A Bishop from Panama discovered the Galapagos Islands.
The Bishop named the islands.

ie, in the second sentence we know which Bishop.

For additional rules on the use of the article check in a simple grammar book.

2

Students work on their own to fill in the gaps. Check the answers round the class, and give additional practice if there are any general problems.

Answers

2 *a* (could also be *the* as *on the beach* is a set expression, like *at the seaside*)
3 *The*
4 *The*
5 *a*
6 *the* (*a church* only if there is more than one, which is unlikely here)
7 *The*
8 *a*
9 *The*
10 *the*

3

You may need to remind your students that in English *the* is not usually used with countries or large geographical features such as lakes or mountains, though it is used with names of rivers. They will find some useful expressions in the passage in Activity 2. Students should complete this exercise in the same way as the previous one.

Answers

1 –   2 *The*   3 *a*   4 *The, the* (we know there is only one cinema)   5 –   6 *an*   7 *a*   8 –   9 *a, the, –*   10 –

4

If your students have difficulty with this exercise, you can give them additional practice from time to time by taking a paragraph from the text book and removing the punctuation – but make sure they do not refer to their books while doing the exercise.

Answers

We went to Australia last year to visit Sharon's family. It was lovely, especially the beaches near the capital city, Sydney. After a few days in the city, we went to Ayers Rock in the centre of the country. The rock is incredible. It's a holy place for the Aborigines and it changes colour when the sun sets.

UNIT 3 LESSON 2

Lesson 2 *Survival at sea*

Aims: To focus on the past simple and pronunciation of the endings; to describe feelings. The topic is a true story of survival at sea.

Language focus

1 Past simple
In 1971 the Robinsons decided to sail around the world.
The whales made holes in the yacht.

2 Pronunciation of past simple endings /ɪd/ /d/ /t/
Killer whales attacked the 'Lucette'.
Water started to come in.

Skills focus

- **Reading:** a text for information, and to follow a story
- **Speaking:** describing feelings

Vocabulary focus

- Nautical items: *life raft, rowing boat, yacht, flare, sail*
- Sea animals: *whale, turtle, shark*
- Survival: *first aid box, to sink, to survive, rescue, drinking water, pills*
- Feeling: *comfortable, confident, depressed, frightened*

Review and Warmer

Tell the students what the topic of this lesson is, and give them a few minutes alone or in pairs to think up some sentences predicting possible events in the story, using superlative adjectives, eg:
The worst moment was when ...
The best day was when ...
They can also use long adjectives, such as *most dangerous, most frightening, most interesting, most beautiful.*

1

Students should work alone or in pairs to do this exercise. The aim of the exercise is to teach unfamiliar vocabulary, so that they can understand the story. They may be able to match some of the words and pictures straight away, but will need to read the text for the others.

Answers
1 *turtle* 2 *shark* 3 *life raft* 4 *killer whale* 5 *yacht*
7 *rowing boat* 8 *sail*
After matching the vocabulary ask students to predict problems you could have when sailing round the world, for example, the weather, sharks, illness or injury.

2

The students now look at the text in more detail to answer the comprehension questions.

Answers
1 *Killer whales made holes in the yacht.*
2 *Six.*
3 *Twelve onions, ten oranges, six lemons, half a kilo of biscuits and some sweets.*

You could look at practice page 73 Language Summary 1 here, and tell the students to do Exercise 1.

3

Ask students to speculate on the next part of the story. They should work in pairs, and not look at their books. If the class find it difficult to get started, you could brainstorm a few suggestions and put them on the board.
Go round monitoring and helping if necessary. If there are any general language problems, deal with them with the whole class afterwards.
After the groups have discussed their ideas, let two or three of them report back to the class. They will find out from the following activity if any of them were correct.

4

Remind students of the use of the article *a* for new information and *the* for something we already know, and point out time expressions used, eg, *from then on, at first, on day 7, after,* to help them with the task. They may find it easier to work in pairs or small groups.
You may need to play the cassette twice for the class to get all the answers in the right order.

Answers

2	3	4	5	6	7	8	9	10
f	k	g	c	a	d	i	e	h

Practice page 73 Exercise 2 would go well here.

5

Ask students how they are feeling at the moment to elicit vocabulary they know for feelings. They then complete the activity, alone or in pairs. Go through the answers with the class. Note that some of the adjectives describe physical feelings, eg, *thirsty*, while others describe mental feelings, eg, *happy*.

Answers
positive feelings: comfortable, confident, excited, happy, relieved
negative feelings: depressed, frightened, lonely, thirsty, tired, uncomfortable, worried
Have a short class discussion on how the people felt, to prepare for the activity. Students should say, eg:
I think they felt frightened when the killer whales attacked the yacht.

16

UNIT 3 LESSON 2

Go round monitoring and helping as necessary. After the groups have compared answers, let some groups report back to the class.
This activity is useful preparation for the homework.

Homework

The activities so far have had only one sentence for each day described. The students should write about four sentences for this paragraph. They could illustrate their diaries for display.

Practice *page 73*

Language Summary 1

This should be revision but it may be worth going through it carefully with the class if they are having problems. Remind them that the past simple is used when a date or time for the action is given, eg, *in 1971, on Day 38.*
There are quite a lot of irregular past tense verbs used in the reading and listening passages in Lesson 2, Activities 1 and 4, so you can refer the students back to them, and replay the cassette if necessary.

1

Students can complete the table on their own and check the answers in pairs.

Answers

present	past
catch	caught
come	came
cut	cut
eat	ate
feel	felt
get	got
have	had
know	knew
light	lit
make	made
put	put
see	saw
sell	sold
sink	sank
take	took

2

Suggest that the students refer to the completed table from Exercise 1 to help them with the past tenses.
Check the answers round the class.

Answers
  2 *They bought a yacht (called 'The Lucette').*
  3 *Whales made holes in the yacht.*
  4 *Water started to come in.*
  5 *Robin and Neil were seasick so Lyn gave them pills (from the first aid box).*
  6 *Sandy caught their first fish (on Day 3).*
  7 *They cut up the fish and 'cooked' it in lemon juice.*
  8 *The family ate raw fish when they had no more lemons.*
  9 *The life raft was always wet so they moved into the rowing boat.*
 10 *Sharks followed them all the time (after Douglas killed the turtle).*
 11 *The family felt (students' choice).*
 12 *Finally a Japanese fishing boat saw their flare.*

Language Summary 2

If you have not done much pronunciation work with your class before, this is a good opportunity to begin. Obtain a chart of the English phonemes if possible. Get the students to put their fingers on their voice box and say the verbs *attack, smell* and *decide*, paying attention to the final sound in each verb (/k/, /l/, /d/).
If the voice box does not vibrate, the consonant is voiceless and the simple past ending pronunciation is /t/. If the voice box vibrates, the consonant is voiced and the end pronunciation is /d/.
Any verbs having a final /d/ or /t/ sound take the pronunciation /ɪd/.
Make sure the students do not voice unvoiced consonants!

3

You may want to do this as a whole class exercise, or have pupils working together in pairs or small groups. If there are general problems, do chorus drills of the words once the table has been completed.
For additional practice the students can pick out all the regular past tense verbs from Lesson 2 Activities 1 and 4.

Answers

/d/	/t/	/ɪd/
dried	liked	corrected
happened	talked	decided
killed	watched	invited
moved		
pulled		
survived		

4

Students should work on their own to do this. They can either check their partner's work, or you could have a competition to see who finishes first, and how many people can get all the opposites correct.

Answers
*after – before   buy – sell   come – go   give – take   happy – sad
positive – negative   raw – cooked   small – large   wet – dry*

UNIT 3 LESSON 3

Lesson 3 *Skeleton Island*

Aims: To learn some prepositions of place to describe features of an island; to use *going to* to talk about future plans and intentions and to make predictions.

Language focus

1 Prepositions of place
The snakes are near the beach.
The swamp is in the south-west of the island.

2 *going to* for future intentions, plans and predictions
What are you going to eat?
We're going to catch fish.

Skills focus

- **Listening:** to a description for true and false statements and so as to complete a map
- **Speaking:** describing and discovering features of an imaginary island through an information gap exercise, and taking part in a group problem-solving activity.

Vocabulary focus

- Animals: *crocodile, snake, piranha*
- Geographical features of an island: *beach, jungle, volcano, mountain, river, swamp*
- Items useful for survival: *a sheet of plastic, mirror, axe, fishing line, nails, hooks, rope*

Review

Either display the students' diary paragraphs, if they have illustrated them, or let students work in pairs to question each other about their day. Monitor for correct use of past simple questions and answers, and give additional practice if there are general problems.

Warmer

Remind the class of the story from Lesson 2, and ask them to imagine the family had landed on an island before they were rescued. Have a brief discussion, in groups or with the whole class, about what they might have found on the island. Groups report their ideas back to the class.

1

This is a vocabulary exercise to prepare for the listening activity. Check the answers with the class.

Answers

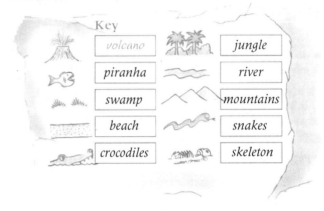

Ask the students to mark the stressed syllables in the vocabulary and check their pronunciation of the words.

2

You may want to go through Language Summary 1 on practice page 74, and do Exercise 1 before you start this activity.
Check the students are familiar with prepositions of place needed for this exercise: *at/in the north* (plus all compass points) *between/around/opposite/in the centre of/in/south of...*).
Give the students time to look at the map so that they can work out where different things are. You could ask them to make sentences saying where everything is, eg:
The volcano is in the centre of the island.
The swamp is in the west of the island.
Particularly for a weaker class, this will make the listening easier.
🔊 Now play the first part of the cassette. You will probably have to play it twice, first for students to find the items, and then for them to check whether the statements are true or false.

Answers
2 *False. The swamp is in the west of the island.*
3 *True.*
4 *True.*
5 *False. The beach is in the north of the island between Sage Bay and Black Rock.*
6 *False. The river runs from the volcano to the inlet.*
7 *True.*

🔊 Students work alone to complete the map while they listen to the second part of the cassette. One way to check the answers is to draw a big map on the board and have two students complete it as they listen. Or you could ask different pairs to come up after the listening is completed and to draw in an item each. You will probably need to play the cassette twice to get all the answers.

3

This is an information gap activity.
Get the students to cover their partner's map with a piece of paper so they don't cheat. Demonstrate the activity with a pair of students using the example given.
Monitor the activity, and afterwards go through any general problems with the class.
You could do practice page 74 Exercise 2 here.

4

Check the students understand the vocabulary by asking them what they could use these items for.
Highlight the use of *going to* to talk about future plans and intentions and to make predictions. You may want to go through Language Summary 2 on practice page 74 here, and tell the class to do Exercise 3 on that page.
Get each student to note down what her/his group decides they are going to do.
If your class is large, you can conduct feedback by cross-grouping the students and getting them to compare their decisions with one member from each of the other groups.

Homework

This should be longer than the homework for Lesson 2, but can follow the same pattern. You may want to brainstorm some ideas with the class and put some ideas on the board. They can also use their ideas from Activity 4 (but the diary will be written in the past simple).

Practice *page 74*

1

Refer students back to Lesson 3 Activities 1, 2 and 3. They should do the exercise alone and compare answers in pairs.

Answers
2 *in front of*   3 *between*   4 *above*
5 *near*   6 *on the left of* 7 *behind*
8 *opposite*   9 *next to*   10 *on*
11 *in*   12 *in the centre of*

2

This gives further practice with prepositions.

Answers
2 *false (He is in the boat.)*
3 *true*
4 *false (It is in front of the tree.)*
5 *false (They are on the hut.)*
6 *false (It is on the left side of the island.)*

Language Summary 2

Refer the students back to Lesson 3 Activity 4.
Go through the examples in the Language Summary. Make sure the students understand that this tense is used for plans and intentions, and also for predictions, ie to talk about things we believe will happen, from our knowledge at the present time. However, they might not happen.
Each student should note down one prediction for the next day, one for the next week, one for the next year, and one for the further future. They can then exchange ideas with their partner. Let some pairs report back to the class, and see if they have the same ideas.

3

This exercise gives controlled practice with *going to*. Students can do it alone and compare answers with their partner.

Answers
2 *He's going to buy some new clothes.*
3 *He's going to have a job interview.*
4 *He's going to visit his mother.*
5 *He's going to write to the bank manager.*
6 *He's going (to go) to a wedding.*
7 *He's going to have dinner with some friends.*
8 *He's going to play football on Saturday.*

The second part of the exercise gives freer practice. Students can exchange ideas with a partner, and some pairs can report back to the class. Monitor and help as necessary.

4

Students can do this exercise alone or in pairs. You may want to do some chorus drilling.

Answers

Country	Nationality
Italy	*Italian*
Germany	*German*
Poland	*Polish*
Scotland	*Scottish (not Scotch – except for whisky)*
Norway	*Norwegian*
Peru	*Peruvian*
Australia	*Australian*
Brazil	*Brazilian*
America	*American*

It is a good idea for students to learn the country and nationality together, and to practise the stress shifts.

Unit 4 Storytelling

The three lessons in this unit are based around the story *The singer not the song*. Students read and listen to the text, performing a variety of tasks to help them follow and develop the story.

Lesson 1 '...our dream's come true'

Aims: To introduce the present perfect simple and to practise *for* and *since* in the context of a developing story.

Language focus

1 Present perfect simple for unfinished past
We've always wanted this chance.
Rob has liked Cindy since he met her.

2 *for* and *since*
We've been working on Rob's new song since Thursday.
We've only worked on my new song for two days.

Skills focus

- **Reading:** a story for detail
- **Listening:** to a passage and comparing it with a written version for differences
- **Speaking:** roleplaying a conversation

Vocabulary focus

- Music: *band, song, agent, record company, studio, guitar, group, concert, manager, to record, record*
- Feelings: *love, nervous, enthusiastic, excited, happy*

Review

Take in the diary paragraphs. Let students read each other's and compare ideas to see if anyone else has written about the same events.

1

Brainstorm around the class for different types of music, eg, jazz, classical, rock, pop, rap, reggae, rock and roll, etc, and write them on the board.
Then you can have a class discussion, a group discussion, or, with a smaller class, students could go round finding about each other's favourite music, and forming groups of people who like the same kind. If time, those groups could then see if there is a favourite artist, composer or group. If you do not have a class discussion, make sure the groups have time to report back to the class.

2

You might want to go through practice page 75 Language Summary 1 before doing Activity 2, if you feel the present perfect is likely to cause problems.
Students should read the first part of the story on their own. They can answer the comprehension questions alone, in pairs or in groups.

Answers
1 Trio. Three: Cindy, Rob and Tony.
2 The chance to make a record.
3 To the manager's office to sign a contract. (Brock is the manager.)
4 Tony. Cindy feels nervous when she's alone with Rob. She puts her arms round Tony.
5 He loves her. When he writes love songs, he thinks of Cindy when he writes the words.

You could go through Language Summary 2 on practice page 75 at this stage, and the students could do Exercise 3.

3

Encourage students to predict what happens next to each character in the story. They should not look at their books at this stage. They should note their suggestions.
Play the cassette for students to see if their predictions were correct. Students listen with books closed to check their predictions.

4

Then students look at the summary and try to correct the mistakes from memory. They can discuss with their partner.
They listen a second time to check.

Answers
Rob has loved Cindy since he met her.
Tony signed the contract.
They are going to the studio on Thursday.
They meet at Cindy's flat.
The song is not perfect.
Rob and Lucy go out to get some Chinese food.
Tony and Cindy listen to the tape.
They both look worried.

5

With a weaker class you might like to brainstorm some ideas with the whole class first. It is a good idea for students to prepare their roles in groups: all the Tonys work together, all the Cindys and all the Lucys. They then get into groups of three to perform the roleplay.
Go round monitoring and helping, but do not stop to correct unless there are real communication problems. At this stage communicating ideas is more important than correct grammar.

UNIT 4 LESSON 1

Homework
Tell the students to write at least ten lines of dialogue involving the three characters. Ask them to check their punctuation carefully. Practice page 75 Exercise 4 gives useful practice in punctuating a dialogue.

Practice *page 75*

Language Summary 1
With a weaker class you may want to go through this carefully and perhaps do some extra practice drills.

1
This exercise focuses on the form of the past participles, which are not always the same as the simple past form for irregular verbs. You could use it as a competition.

Answers

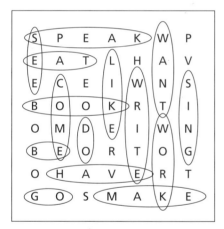

book	booked	make	made
come	come	see	seen
do	done	sing	sung
eat	eaten	speak	spoken
go	gone	want	wanted
have	had	work	worked
like	liked	write	written

2
This is controlled practice with one common use of the present perfect. *Ever* has the meaning of 'in your life', 'up to now'. You could pair students up to ask and answer the questions.

Answers
2 *Have you ever written a song?*
3 *Have you ever eaten Chinese food?*
4 *Have you ever sung in a group?*
5 *Have you ever been on TV?*
6 *Have you ever spoken to a pop star?*
7 *Have you ever played the guitar?*
8 *Have you ever seen a pop concert?*

Language Summary 2
These two words sometimes give learners problems. Both are used to speak about how long something has been happening, but *for* is used with a period of time, and *since* is followed by a point in time. Note that this may not be expressed as a date or time, but may be a verb phrase, eg *I've lived here since I came to London.*
Refer students back to the texts in Lesson 1, and tell them to find all the examples of *for* and *since*, and to note the verbs used with them.

3
This exercise should be done by the students on their own and then checked in pairs or round the class.

Answers
3 *since 1989*
4 *for a long time*
5 *since they started singing*
6 *since she was a child*
7 *for two weeks*
8 *since last Friday*
9 *for weeks*
10 *since this morning*

4
This exercise will be useful preparation for the homework in Lesson 1. Make sure students do not refer to their books while they do it. They can check Cindy's part on Student's Book page 24, picture 5.

Answers
Tony: No, Cindy, it's not a dream. We've always wanted to make a record, and this time our dream's come true! We're going into the recording studio next week!

UNIT 4 LESSON 2

Lesson 2 *Cindy's crisis*

Aim: To use *should* for advice and *have got to* for obligation while continuing to follow the story begun in the previous lesson.

Language focus

1 Advice: *should/shouldn't*
You should go out more.
You shouldn't be so selfish.

2 Obligation: *have got to*
You've got to start living again.
You've got to help Tony.

Skills focus

- **Listening:** to a story for detail
- **Reading:** a story for detail and to look for advice given
- **Speaking:** retelling a story and giving advice

Vocabulary focus

- Feelings: *to feel fine, a shock, awful, selfish*
- Relationships: *kiss, to cry, to talk, to listen, to need help, to leave someone alone, to give advice, problem*

Review

Ask for volunteers or nominate students to roleplay the dialogues they wrote for the Lesson 1 homework. There probably won't be time to roleplay everyone's dialogue, but ensure that all the students have the opportunity to speak.

1

You may want to start the class off by asking a few general questions, eg, the names of the characters and the group, and writing the answers on the board. Students should do this without looking at their books.

2

▣ Tell students to read through the sentences first to help them focus on the listening.

Answers
2 *true*
3 *false – A car hit him.*
4 *false – He's dead.*
5 *true*
6 *true*
7 *false – They don't go.*
8 *false – She still feels awful.*

3

You may want to highlight the structure *should (not)* + infinitive without *to* to give advice, and refer to Language Summary 1 on practice page 76. *Have got to* + infinitive to express obligation is covered in Language Summary 2 on the same page.
Students could speculate on the answers before they read the next part of the story, and then see whether they were right.

Answers
Lucy advises Cindy to go out more, not to be so selfish, and to think about other people.
The students will have their own opinions as to whether the advice is good. They can discuss this in pairs or small groups, and then report back to the class, giving their reasons if they can.

4

Exercises 1 and 2 on practice page 76 would go well here, and Language Summary 1, if you have not already covered it.
Pairs can join with other pairs to compare their advice, and then report back to the class, to see how many give the same advice.
This activity is useful preparation for the homework, so make sure students take notes.

5

As a recycling activity for Unit 3 Lesson 2, ask the students which of these verbs are regular and which are irregular, and how the regular verb endings are pronounced – are they /t/, /d/ or /ɪd/?
Regular: kissed /t/, remembered /d/, started /ɪd/, listened /d/
Irregular: met (meet), told (tell), ran (run)
The students can work in pairs and try to guess the order of the events before they listen.
▣ You may need to play the cassette twice or three times for students to get the order right.

Answers

2	3	4	5	6	7	8
a	d	h	b	g	e	c

UNIT 4 LESSON 2

6

Briefly explain the layout for an informal letter, position of the date, address and salutation. There is an example of an informal letter in Unit 1 Lesson 3 Activity 4.
You may need to start the letter on the board, eg:
Dear (name)
I have a problem and I want to ask for your advice.
Yesterday I saw Tony again and ...
Tell students to tell Cindy's story in their own words using the simple past and present perfect, perhaps ending with the question *What should I do?* or *Can you give me some advice?* Remind students that they will answer this letter for their homework.

Homework

You may want to brainstorm some suggestions and put them on the board. Tell students to refer to the advice they gave in Activity 4. They could also refer to practice page 76, Exercise 1.

Practice *page 76*

Language Summary 1

Refer students back to Lesson 2 Activity 3. If you think it is useful, tell them to go through the story noting all the examples of *should/shouldn't* for advice.

1

This is a controlled exercise in recognition of the structure. It uses ideas from the story.

Answers
  A – 2   B – 3   C – 1

2

This is a controlled production exercise. Students could do it orally in pairs before writing the answers.

Answers
  3 *You shouldn't smoke.* or *You should stop smoking.*
  4 *You should have/take a holiday.*
  5 *You shouldn't drink so much coffee.* or *You should stop drinking coffee.*
  6 *You shouldn't eat cakes.* or *You should stop eating cakes.*

Language Summary 2

Deal with this in the same way as Language Summary 1.

3

The first part of this is also a controlled exercise which the students can do alone and check with their partners.

Answers
  2 *Brock has (got) to write a new contract.*
  3 *Tony and Cindy have (got) to go to the recording studio.*
  4 *The police have (got) to interview Lucy.*
  5 *Cindy has (got) to meet Tony.*
  6 *Tony has (got) to find another person for the band.*

UNIT 4 LESSON 3

Lesson 3 'I can't live without your love'

Aims: To make predictions about how the story will end, and to learn personal pronouns and possessive adjectives.

Language focus

1 *will* for predictions
I think Cindy will sing with Tony.
I think Tony will make a record without Cindy.

2 pronouns and possessive adjectives
I can't live without your love.
He'll be nervous on his own.
Is this guitar yours?

Skills focus

- **Reading:** the next part of the story
- **Speaking:** making predictions about the story
- **Listening:** for detail, and to check the predictions
- **Writing:** a song

Vocabulary focus

- **Feelings:** *to change one's mind, to be pleased for someone*
- **Music:** *to go on a tour, to go solo, to be successful, concert*

Review and Warmer

Ask the class to tell the story so far, a sentence for each student. Then ask them to say briefly what they think each person (Lucy, Cindy, Tony) should do next.

1

Help students with the task by getting them to focus on the pronouns in the text bubbles. You may want to go through Language Summary 2 on practice page 77 at this stage. Students can work alone or in pairs.

Answers
b–8 c–7 d–6 e–1 f–2 g–3 h–5

🔊 You may need to play the cassette twice for students to get all the speech bubbles in the right place.
You could tell the class to do practice page 77 Exercise 4 here.

2

Students work in small groups of three or four. They should all note down their version of how the story ends. You can then cross-group the students to form new groups (with one person from each original group) to compare their versions before listening.

🔊 After they have listened to the last part of the story, ask how many were right about the ending.
Language Summary 1 and Exercise 1 on practice page 77 would go well here.

3

Students are asked to speculate beyond the text. You could brainstorm some ideas to start the discussion.
Go round monitoring the groups, noting how they use *will* for making predictions, and checking on correct use of personal pronouns and possessive adjectives, but do not interrupt the flow of ideas. If necessary, do remedial work afterwards.

4

This is a fun exercise. Students may want to base their words on a tune they already know, or adapt a song they already know.
If time is short, this could be done for homework. Any good songs could be displayed round the classroom, or if you have any musical students, they could perform for the class.

Homework

Remind students of the dialogue they wrote for their homework in Unit 4 Lesson 1, for the style and punctuation. You may want to prepare the dialogue in class, or brainstorm some ideas.
Tell the students to check their work carefully before handing it in. They should check their grammar, spelling, punctuation, vocabulary and content structure.

Practice *page 77*

1

You may need to remind students of the negative form, *won't*. They should do the exercise alone and correct it with a partner.

Answers
3 *will be*
4 *'ll/will buy*
5 *will be*
6 *will lose*
7 *won't be*
8 *'ll/will do*
9 *'ll/will have*
10 *will feel*
11 *won't have to*

UNIT 4 LESSON 3

2

You may wish to brainstorm a few ideas from the class before students write their own opinions. Or students can just use the ideas from Exercise 1. To extend the activity, let students discuss their ideas in pairs or small groups, or have a class discussion. See if you can get class agreement on any ideas about the future.

3

This is a good opportunity to do some pronunciation practice of vowels. You could extend the practice by getting students to find other words for each sound. Have a competition to see how many different spellings of the same sound each pair or small group can find.
Students should say the words to their partner. Go round monitoring, and check the answers with the class.

Answers
3 – S   4 – S   5 – D   6 – S   7 – S   8 – D

4

Possessive pronouns can cause problems, particularly *mine*, which has no -*s*, and *its*, which has no apostrophe, but this should be revision for your students. If you think it will be useful, tell the class to go through the texts from Lesson 3 and pick out all the possessive adjectives and pronouns, noting how they are used. They can complete the table on their own or as a class exercise.

Answers

subject pronouns	object pronouns	possessive adjectives	possessive pronouns
I	*me*	my	*mine*
you	you	*your*	yours
he	*him*	his	*his*
she	her	*her*	hers
it	*it*	its	*its*
we	us	*our*	ours
they	*them*	their	*theirs*

5

Students should be able to do this exercise easily once they have completed the table in Exercise 4, so you may want to do it orally with the whole class.

Answers
1 *your, mine, yours*   2 *your, Their, it*   3 *hers, Her*
4 *them, their, it*   5 *they*

6

This is another fun activity, which you can use as a team competition. You can always use word squares to practise new vocabulary, and students can make their own to exchange with a partner.

Answers

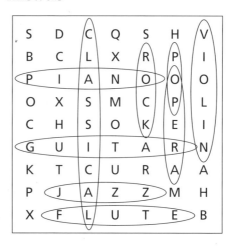

25

Unit 5 Family life

The theme for this unit is families, in particular, large and small families, male and female family roles, family customs in different countries, and rules for children.

Lesson 1 *What size family?*

Aim: To give students practice in reading and talking about different sized families, and in expressing advantages and disadvantages.

Language focus

1 Zero conditional: *if* + present simple + present simple
If they go anywhere as a family, they need two cars.
Present simple + *if* + present simple
The children spend too long on the phone if he doesn't watch.

2 Talking about advantages and disadvantages
One advantage/disadvantage of + -ing/noun + is that ...
One advantage of being an only child is that you get lots of presents.

Skills focus

- **Reading:** a magazine article to get specific information and main ideas for discussion
- **Speaking:** discussing advantages and disadvantages
- **Listening:** to a personal opinion for specific information

Vocabulary focus

- Adjectives of personality: *bored, careful, hard-working*
- Family relationships: *cousin, nephew, niece, aunt, uncle*
- Clothes: *jacket, shirt, trousers*
- Rooms in a house: *hall, attic, dining room, bedroom*

Review

At the beginning of the lesson you could spend the first few minutes on proof reading the dialogues students wrote for their homework in Unit 4 Lesson 3. Students read each other's dialogues and mark in pencil any errors for the writer to correct. Or you could pair students to act out their homework dialogues.

Warmer

Ask students to bring in photos of families and/or friends. Then in groups get them to talk about the people and the occasion of the photo(s). Or ask students to bring in an unnamed photo of them as a baby or young child. Number and display the photos round the room and in pairs the students try and identify them all.

1

Students do this alone, then check the answers in pairs. Go round monitoring and helping as necessary. Encourage them to guess the meaning of unknown words from context, using the picture to help.

Answers
2 – *a*   3 – *h*   4 – *c*   5 – *j*

2

After the students have done the adjective exercise in pairs, elicit the answers, and check the pronunciation, writing the adjectives up on the board under three column headings, *positive, negative,* and *both.*
Several of the adjectives can be both. Tell students to give reasons if they disagree.
Before the students read the article, identify Richard and Janet as the parents in the picture.

Answers
Richard: careful, fair, hard-working, strict
Janet: lonely, bored, fair, hard-working, strict
Sarah: hard-working
Victoria: lazy

Ask the students to give reasons for the adjectives, eg:
Janet was lonely when she was a child, and her life was dull (ie she was bored).
Richard and Janet try to be fair with the children.
Students read the questions following the text before they read the text again. They compare answers in pairs.

Answers
Christopher and Sarah have bedrooms of their own. Janet was an only child.

3

Encourage the students to think up some ideas of their own as well as using the text. Collect the answers on the board.

Possible answers

advantages	disadvantages
never lonely	no privacy
others to play with/talk to	no space
learn to share	hard work for the parents
can help each other	clothes handed down
community spirit	difficult for children to get attention
	more arguments

There are some examples of the zero conditional in the text, and if your students find them difficult to understand, you could go through Language Summary 1 on practice page 78 at this stage.

UNIT 5 LESSON 1

4

Ask students to speculate about Debra's family background in pairs, using the photo and the statements. Explain *to make a fuss over someone* = to give someone a lot of attention. They should be able to work out that Debra was an only child. When they report back, get them to give reasons for their decision.

▣ Play the cassette through once. You may need to play it a second time for them to get all the statements and adjectives. You may also need to explain the difference between *imaginative* (an imaginative person pictures things in their mind that are not real) and *imaginary* (not real).

Answers
Debra makes statements 2, 4, 5, 6, 7.
Adjectives: lonely, spoilt, imaginative

5

If you want to exploit the listening passage more, get the students to listen again, and note down any other information about Debra.
For the group discussion encourage the students to compare the Astons' and Debra's family experiences first before they move on to their own. Perhaps extend the activity and get the students to choose which adjectives in Activity 2 applied to them as children, and now. You could extend the list of adjectives first.

Homework

Language Summary 2 on practice page 78 gives further examples of using this structure. If students need more preparation, get them to write full sentences for the advantages/disadvantages written in table form for Activity 3, eg:
One advantage of being in a large family is that children learn to share.

Practice *page 78*

Language Summary 1

Refer students back to the text in Lesson 1 Activity 3. They could pick out all the examples of the zero conditional.

1

Students can work alone or in pairs. Check the answers round the class.

Answers
2 *has breakfast*   3 *is late*
4 *cycles to work*   5 *is bad*
6 *starts work*   7 *has lunch*
8 *is busy*   9 *leaves work*
10 *go to the park*   11 *go home*

2

In each sentence in this exercise, the *if* clause could go second. Point out that *if* could be replaced by *when* in these sentences.

Answers
2 *If the weather's bad, I stay at home.* or *I stay at home if the weather's bad.*
3 *If my parents go on holiday, I look after the house.*
4 *If I feel tired, I don't go jogging.*
5 *If my friend Samina stays, we go camping.*
6 *If the weather is good, I cycle to work.*

Students work in pairs to ask and answer the next questions.

3

This could be done as a group competition to see how many advantages/disadvantages for each question each group could come up with that are different from the other groups' answers.

Possible answers
2 *One advantage of living in a city is that there is a lot of entertainment.*
One disadvantage of living in a city is that there is a lot of noise/pollution/traffic.
3 *One advantage of working at night is that you have free time during the day.*
One disadvantage of working at night is that it is difficult to socialize.
4 *One advantage of travelling by bus is that it is fairly cheap.*
One disadvantage of travelling by bus is that it is sometimes inconvenient.
5 *One advantage of shopping in a market is that the food is cheaper.*
One disadvantage of shopping in a market is that the quality of food/clothes is not always good.

4

This exercise could be done in pairs or as a competition.

Answers
living room – The TV is usually in this room.
hall – The room near the front door.
toilet – The smallest room in the house.
dining room – The room where you eat your meals.
bathroom – You can have a shower here.
kitchen – The cooking is done here.

UNIT 5 LESSON 2

Lesson 2 *House rules*

Aims: To give students practice in talking about and listening to childhood experiences, and to give them practice in expressing their opinions on discipline in the home.

Language focus

1 *be allowed to* and *could* for permission compared with *have to* for obligation
I was allowed to drink wine at dinner but I wasn't allowed to smoke.
I could eat sweets between meals, and I didn't have to eat all my dinner.

2 *Make* or *do*
having to make your bed every day
having to do your homework every evening

Skills focus

- **Speaking:** talking about family life in general, and about personal experiences in the past
- **Listening:** to personal experiences about childhood for specific information

Vocabulary focus

- Household tasks: *to make the bed, do the ironing, clean the house, do the washing up, do the cooking, do the shopping*

Review

You could hold a class survey to see which students prefer being an only child or a member of a big family. Students discuss their reasons in groups of up to six. The groups then report back. Finally the class decide on the three or four main advantages and disadvantages of being an only child or a member of a big family. This activity takes in the homework for Unit 5 Lesson 1.

Warmer

Ask the students to think of something they had to do at home when they were a child and tell another student.
Or tell the students to draw, on a small piece of paper, two things that remind them of their childhood and discuss them in groups.

Or ask the students to write down, on separate pieces of paper, the name of a place, a date, and an object that were of special significance in their childhood. Put the students in groups. Tell them to mix their pieces of paper and put them in a pile face down in the middle of the group. They turn the pieces of paper over one at a time, and the student who has written that particular one explains the significance of their date/object/place to the others.

1

You will probably need to explain *allowed to, could* and *have to* before the students do the activity. You could start by going through the Language Summary on practice page 79.
Or let the students have a discussion while you monitor them. Write up some of the common errors on the board and do an error correction as a lead in to the grammar.
Encourage students to give reasons for their opinions, eg:
'No eating sweets' is a good idea because sweets are bad for your teeth.
If students ask, *a snack* = something small to eat between meals, such as a sandwich, a bar of chocolate; *swearing* = saying rude words.
Practice page 79 Exercises 1 and 2 would fit in well here, or after Activity 2.

2

This activity is similar to the previous one, and can be dealt with in the same way.
You could put pairs of students into groups of four for a discussion of Activities 1 and 2.

3

Pause the cassette between Jane's and Brendan's texts. Let the students compare answers in pairs. When eliciting the answers from the students encourage them to give their answers in full sentences in the past, eg:
Jane wasn't allowed to leave the house without permission.
Remind them to listen for the speaker's opinion of having strict parents.

Answers

J: No playing with children in the street.
Always having to ask for permission to go out.
Always coming home on time.
She didn't think having strict parents was a good thing.

B: No eating snacks or sweets between meals.
Having to eat all your dinner.
He thought having strict parents was probably a good thing.

UNIT 5 LESSON 2

4

Get a spokesperson from each group to summarize their predicted story to the rest of the class. Use the photo to get students to predict what a hippie is. (*Hippie* = person who rejects organized society and social conventions, wears unusual and colourful clothes, and may live in a community with other hippies.)

🔊 Play the cassette once and let the students discuss in their groups what they think happened. They should use the words in the box to help them.

Then play the cassette again and allow further discussion. Get each group to choose a different spokesperson to tell part of the story to the whole class.

Encourage groups to correct each other. Which group had the most details correct? Which group's predicted story was closest to the truth?

5

You could extend the discussion to students' opinions of strict parents, and what they think of the law in several countries that it is illegal to hit a child.

Homework

Suggest the students write about one of the occasions they have just told their partner about. Ask them to write about 100 words.

Practice *page 79*

Language Summary

Refer students back to Lesson 2 Activities 1 and 2. Go through the examples in the Language Summary. If your students have problems, you may need to drill the structures.

1

Students could complete this exercise alone and then compare answers in pairs. Tell them to read the whole dialogue before they try to fill in the gaps.

Answers
2 *were allowed to/could buy*
3 *weren't allowed to/couldn't do*
4 *weren't allowed to/couldn't play*
5 *allowed to go out*
6 *had to be (or come)*
7 *was allowed to/could go out*
8 *didn't have to/come (or be)*
9 *had to do*
10 *was allowed to/could visit*
11 *was allowed to/could watch*
12 *didn't have to help*

2

Students complete this exercise alone or in pairs. Extend the activity by getting them to write sentences about themselves.

Answers
2 *Dave wasn't allowed to/couldn't play football.*
3 *Sue and Dave had to do their homework.*
4 *Dave was allowed to/could ride a motorbike.*
5 *Sue and Dave were not allowed to/couldn't smoke.*
6 *Sue was allowed to/could watch TV.*

3

Students could use a dictionary to help them with this exercise.
Extend the activity by getting them to think of other phrases they know using *make* or *do*.

Answers

make	do
a cake, a mistake, a noise, a suggestion	the cooking, your homework, the ironing, the shopping, the washing, the washing up

4

Students complete this exercise alone or in pairs. Check the answers round the class.
The only way to learn the use of these words successfully is to encourage students to learn set phrases with *make* and *do*, and to give them mini tests from time to time.

Answers
2 *do*   3 *doing*   4 *do*
5 *make*   6 *do*   7 *making*
8 *make*

29

UNIT 5 LESSON 3

Lesson 3 *Family roles*

Aim: To give students practice in discussing family roles in different countries and expressing their opinions.

Language focus

Adverbs of frequency
The father usually goes out to work.
Marriage between people from different cultures is always difficult.
Men don't usually spend enough time with their children.

Skills focus

- **Speaking:** discussing family roles and interviewing someone
- **Listening:** to personal opinions for specific information
- **Writing:** questions in preparation for an interview and a newspaper article about family life

Vocabulary focus

- Relationships: *marriage, wedding, divorce, living together, couple, relatives*

Review

Ask students in groups of three or four to agree on a list of between five and ten house rules to display on a poster on the wall. They then look at the other groups' posters and decide which would be the strictest and the least strict household.
Or you could ask the whole class or groups to write up and present on a poster a list of class rules, eg:
You must only speak English.
You are not allowed to smoke in class.
They could include some suggested punishments, which will probably be amusing, or involve 'forfeits' such as reciting something in English to the class.

Warmer

This could act as a warmer for any of the three lessons in this unit. Write up on the board the following quotation from the opening of the Russian writer Tolstoy's novel *Anna Karenina*: 'All happy families resemble one another, but each unhappy family is unhappy in its own way.'
Ask students to discuss in pairs or groups whether they agree and if so, what they think makes a family happy or unhappy.

1

This activity could be done in pairs or, with a smallish class, as an 'onion ring' discussion.

Half the students sit in a circle facing outwards. The other half sit opposite someone, in a circle facing inwards. Let the students discuss the first (and possibly second) statement(s) for a few minutes. Then you say 'Change' and all the students in the outer circle move on one place clockwise to face a new discussion partner. You keep moving the students on every few minutes until the majority have discussed all the statements. Make sure students give their reasons.
If your students do the activity in pairs, ask one or two pairs to report back to the class for each statement, and see whether the class as a whole agrees or disagrees.

2

Note: The ideas expressed by Ida (Italian) in Activities 2 and 3, and Jan (half British, half Norwegian) in Activity 4 are their own personal views and generalizations that obviously many other people from Italy and Norway may disagree with. The aim of these viewpoints is to stimulate discussion, not to give the impression that this is 'the truth' about these countries.
If students are struggling for ideas, get them to use the topic list as a prompt. One person in each group acts as secretary and writes down the ideas so that they can compare their ideas with Ida's after listening to the cassette. Get each group to share one or two of their ideas with the whole class.
▶ Play the cassette once. If the class are really having problems, play it again, stopping after each topic is mentioned.

Answers

1 *role of the father*   2 *role of the mother*
3 *children*   4 *living together*
5 *marriage*   6 *divorce*
7 *single parents*   8 *old relatives*

3

Let the students read through the alternatives. They may need reminding now of the differences in the adverbs of frequency in order to do the listening task. Use the Language Summary and Exercise 1 on practice page 80 as preparation.
The other phrase necessary for the listening is *tend to do*.
▶ Play the cassette once and let students compare answers in their groups. Then play the cassette again if necessary.
Give time for students to check their predictions with Ida's ideas and discuss what they disagree with, or are surprised about. Some individuals can report back to the class.

Answers

1 – *a*   2 – *c*   3 – *b*   4 – *b*   5 – *b*   6 – *b*   7 – *a*   8 – *a*

4

Either keep the same groups, or put the students into new groups. Tell them to write down their ideas again.
▶ Then do the next listening comprehension, playing the cassette twice if necessary.
Finally students discuss Jan's answers, comparing them with their own ideas. Again a few individuals report to the class.

Answers

1 – b   2 – b   3 – a   4 – a   5 – b   6 – a   7 – b
8 – a (in rural communities) b (in the city)
Practice page 80 Exercise 2 would fit in well here.

5

Students could discuss in pairs or in the same groups. Encourage them to make comparisons between the two countries, eg:
It seems that the divorce rate is higher in Norway than in Italy.
Parents seem stricter in Italy than in Norway.
If necessary, refer to Unit 2, Lesson 3 for comparatives.
As before, ask some pairs to report back to the class.
You could extend the activity by asking students to tick the boxes in Activity 3 for their own country. They could also compare Italy and Norway with their own country. If you have students from either of those countries, ask if they agree or disagree with Ida and Jan.

6

You could leave this interview open to cover any aspect of family life covered in this unit, or limit it to a particular focus. If families could prove a delicate topic for some students, a more general interview on attitudes, such as those in Activity 1, would be more appropriate.
Give time for students to prepare questions in pairs. Correct the grammar. If students take a long time writing questions you may need to postpone the interview until the next lesson. Students take notes on their partners' answers, or, if possible, they could record the interviews and make notes from the recordings.
This activity is good preparation for the homework. However, remind students to write notes at this stage, not full sentences.

Homework

As preparation, do part of an article on Ida and Jan on the board, accepting contributions from the class. Start by eliciting some imaginary background information from students, eg:
Yesterday I interviewed Ida Cirillo in her home in Rome. Ida is ... She lives with ... She works as a ... She has ... children and she is very strict. They are not allowed to ... , but they can ...

Practice page 80

1

Refer students back to Lesson 3 Activity 3.
Draw the scale on the board and elicit the answers. Note that *frequently* and *often* mean much the same.

Answers

always, usually, often, frequently, sometimes, occasionally, rarely, never

2

Students do this exercise alone or in pairs.
If the students all come from the same country you could get them to write their three sentences on pieces of paper or card to be displayed round the classroom. Students then go round the class in pairs correcting the grammar and commenting on any sentences they disagree with.

Answers

2 *In Italy a girl often has to ask permission to go out.*
3 *In Italy people rarely get divorced.*
4 *Parents in Norway are not usually strict.*
5 *Parents in Britain are occasionally strict.*
6 *In Norway the father sometimes stays at home with the children.*
7 *In Britain couples frequently do the shopping together.*
8 *In Britain people don't always get married in a church.*
9 *People frequently spend too much money on weddings.*
10 *A second marriage usually lasts longer than a first marriage in Britain.*

3

This is quite difficult so students should work in pairs. Point out that they should rewrite the sentence using the same verb form as in the original sentence.
Vocabulary: *to afford to do something* = to have enough money to do something.

Answers

2 *I usually visit my parents on Sundays.*
3 *I have occasionally been late for work.*
4 *I have rarely been to the doctor.*
5 *My friend Mario is sometimes able to help me.*
    or *My friend Mario can sometimes help me.*
6 *My sister can't usually afford to go on holiday.*
    or *My sister can rarely afford to go on holiday.*
7 *When I was a child I wasn't usually allowed to play outside.*
8 *In my home town people always went to Mass on Sunday.*
9 *I have rarely tried to give up smoking.*
10 *I never made my bed when I was young.*

This could be extended into an oral activity in pairs. Student As say six sentences about themselves. Some should be true and some false, eg:
I always drink coffee for breakfast.
I have never been late for work.
Student Bs have to guess whether each sentence is true or false. Then the students reverse roles and count how many they guessed correctly.

4

Encourage the students to read the whole text before filling in the gaps.

Answers

1 *family*   2 *married*   3 *Marriage*
4 *divorce*   5 *living together* 6 *breaks up*
7 *children*   8 *relatives*

Unit 6 Time

The theme of this unit is time. The first lesson is about a murder mystery which happened in 1926; the other two lessons focus on events in the past and their relation to the present or the future.

Lesson 1 *Murder at Château Firenze*

Aims: To focus on describing past events, talking about what was happening at a specific time or when something else happened and to stimulate discussion about who did what, when and why.
The story is a murder mystery set in 1926. There is no clear answer to who the murderer is. It could be any of the suspects.

Language focus

1 Past continuous and past simple
I was reading when I heard three shots.
I was looking at the body when Lady Francesca came in.

2 *anybody, nobody, somebody, everybody*
There was nobody there.
There wasn't anybody else in the room.

3 Past simple passive (for recognition only)
Three shots were heard.
The body of Sir Dennis was found in the library.

4 Expressions of doubt and certainty, and giving reasons
I'm sure it was ... because...
Perhaps/maybe it was ... because...

Skills focus

- **Reading:** an interview for detail and to make notes
- **Listening:** to interviews for detail and to make notes
- **Speaking:** discussing facts and possibilities
- **Writing:** reporting events in an informal letter

Vocabulary focus

- Crime: *police, interview, murder, detective, clue, shot, gun*
- Occupations: *businessman, artist, lawyer, art dealer, collector, fashion designer, athlete*
- Features of a house: *terrace, games room, study, summer-house, path, French window, lake*

Review

Unit 5 Lesson 3 Activity 1 could be extended into a class survey, and all the results could be tabulated and reported, eg:
Most people agree that ...
Only one person thinks that ...

1

You could first brainstorm famous detectives and detective story writers (eg Agatha Christie with Hercule Poirot and Miss Marple; Georges Simenon with Maigret, etc). Students in pairs tell the story of a detective film or book they have seen or read recently. Useful vocabulary: *victim, suspect* (noun), *suspect* (verb), *criminal, crime.*

2

The Château murder is set in 1926. Ask the students to look at the plan and the pictures. Check vocabulary, eg *study, games room* (for playing snooker, billiards, cards, etc), *French windows, summer-house, château* (French word also used in English). What happened? The past simple passive occurs here for recognition only and with only two verbs: *were heard* and *was found.*
The characters: this is a 'period' murder so all the characters are rich and aristocratic. Don't worry about the pronunciation of the names.
Students should read through as quickly as they can, as they do not need too much detail at this stage. They can then discuss the questions in pairs and report back to the class, or form groups with other pairs and discuss with them.
You could do a quick quiz game with the students' books shut: who's who, what rooms are there in the château, etc? Do this either as a whole class or let the students test each other in pairs.

3

The class either read silently and make notes on their own, or they could work in small groups with one student reading one character's text only. The groups then come together to compare answers.
You may like to go through one character with the whole class and complete a table on the board with three headings:

Who?	Where?	What doing?
Lady Francesca	in the library	reading
Max de Selles	in the games room	playing cards
Agnes Johansson	on the terrace	drinking whisky and reading
the Contessa	in the garden	walking

This would be a good place to go through practice page 81 Language Summary 1 and Exercise 2.

4

Students work alone or in pairs to draw the characters' movements on the plan. You may like to do a rough sketch on the board and go through one character's movements with the class, filling in the movements on your plan.

UNIT 6 LESSON 1

Answers

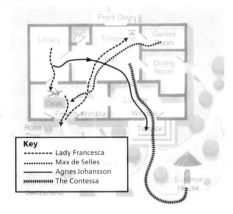

You may want students to describe the movements as they fill in the plan. Exercise 4 on practice page 81 gives practice with prepositions and could be done here.
Encourage the students, in pairs or groups, to speculate on who did it and why. If necessary give them expressions such as *I think it was/I'm sure it was/Maybe it was/Perhaps it was ... because*

5

🔊 The listening extracts are fairly brief. Play them once with the students' books closed, then two or three times more as necessary while students make notes, working alone or in pairs.
Remind them that for notes they just need to focus on the main points. Go round monitoring and helping as necessary.

6

Make sure students give reasons for their deductions. You may need to go through the example suggestions first, or discuss one character with the class.
After the pairs have discussed their ideas with other pairs, some groups report their conclusions back to the class. Who is the favoured suspect? Who is the least likely suspect?
This discussion is useful preparation for the homework, so encourage students to make notes on their conclusions.
You could roleplay interviews in pairs between Sherlock Holmes and a suspect. Get the students to prepare questions first, then do the roleplay.
A possible solution to the murder is that it was Lady Francesca. The Contessa was Sir Dennis's daughter and he was going to tell her this in the unfinished letter and change his will. Lady Francesca suspected this, saw the letter and shot him. She secretly blamed Sir Dennis for her parents' death because he'd been flying the plane.

Homework

This is an informal letter to Dr Watson describing the murder and the murderer briefly (maximum 150-200 words). You may want to suggest students invent new 'facts' to support their case. Refer them to the informal letter layout in Unit 1 Lesson 3. The finished and corrected letters could be displayed in the classroom.

Practice *page 81*

Language Summary 1

Ask students to find examples of the past simple and the past continuous in the reading and listening texts in Lesson 1.

1

Then get students to do Exercise 1 individually or in pairs. They will need to make questions in the past continuous to find out information for the true sentences about other students.
Ask some pairs to report back to the class about their partners.

2

If necessary, point out that the verb *to be* is rarely used in the continuous form. If students read out the dialogue, point out the unmarked forms of *was* and *were* (/wəz/ /wə/) in connected speech.

Answers

2 *was*   3 *was working*   4 *Did you hear*
5 *heard*   6 *were*   7 *were arguing*
8 *were you*   9 *was drinking*   10 *came in*
11 *was crying*

Language Summary 2

Start by asking students to find the examples in the texts in Lesson 1. Note that there is both a *someone* and a *somebody*. Point out that all the indeterminate pronouns *everybody*, *somebody* etc. have equivalents ending in *-one*. They mean the same.

3

Students could work on their own and check their answers in pairs. You could ask some pairs to read the dialogue to the class.

Answers

2 *somebody*   3 *anybody*   4 *everybody*   5 *everybody*
6 *Nobody*   7 *everybody*

4

Start by asking students to find the prepositions of direction in the texts in Lesson 1. Check the matching exercise before the students complete the text. They can work on their own or in pairs, and check the answers in pairs or round the class.

Answers

1 *into*   2 *round*   3 *along*   4 *through*   5 *across*
6 *down*   7 *up*

2 *up*   3 *down*   4 *into*   5 *through*   6 *into*
7 *along*   8 *round*   9 *round*   10 *into*

33

UNIT 6 LESSON 2

Lesson 2 *Time capsules*

Aims: To focus on reporting past events, and to stimulate discussion on what things illustrate life today. This lesson focuses on the simple past passive and the topic of time capsules, both old (pyramids) and new, two similar contexts in that they are both ways of preserving things for the future, and should provide plenty of discussion when the students plan their own time capsule.

Language focus

1 Past simple passive
The Pyramids were built thousands of years ago.
We know how the Great Pyramid was built.

2 Determiners: *a, an, some*
It contained a broken wine bottle, some Victorian money and a newspaper.

3 Suggestions: *What about ...? How about ...? Let's ...*

Skills focus

- **Reading:** a text about the Pyramids for detail
- **Listening:** to a news programme for gist and for specific language
- **Speaking:** Making suggestions and giving reasons
- **Writing:** a newspaper article

Vocabulary focus

- Pyramids: *quarry, block of stone, after-life, tomb, bodies, passage, tunnel*
- Occupations: *archaeologist, robber, servant, worker, builder, pupil, teacher*

Review

Either display the letters the students wrote from Sherlock Holmes, or let them read each other's letters in groups. Then discuss possible solutions to the mystery. See if you can reach class agreement.

Warmer

If possible ask the students the lesson before to find out three facts about the ancient Egyptians. Then let them compare their findings in class. If this is not possible, brainstorm in class what the students know about the ancient Egyptians.

1

The photo is of the Great Pyramid of Cheops, built between 1668 and 1690 BC on the west bank of the Nile.

2

If you have not already done so, brainstorm what the class knows about the ancient Egyptians, and put the ideas on the board. Pyramids are sure to be mentioned. The students then work in pairs to answer the statements. Make sure they do not look at the text until they have tried to answer all the questions.
Vocabulary: students may have difficulty pronouncing the words *quarry* – /ˈkwɒrɪ/, *archaeologist* – /ˌɑːkɪˈɒlədʒɪst/, and *pharaoh* – /ˈfeərəʊ/.
Make sure students give evidence from the text to justify their decisions.

Answers

1 *true*
2 *false: 'Archaeologists are not totally sure how the Great Pyramid was built.'*
3 *true*
4 *true*
5 *false: 'no bodies were ever discovered in them.'*

3

Students work either on their own or in pairs. Tell them to guess the meanings of words they do not know from context. Check the answers with the whole class.

Answers

1 – c   2 – d   3 – f   4 – a   5 – b   6 – e

4

Students should re-read the text looking for expressions of uncertainty. If they have problems, tell them to look for key phrases, eg, *Archaeologists are not totally sure how the Great Pyramid was built.*

Answers

How the Great Pyramid was built (Archaeologists are not totally sure); *how the blocks were transported* (some people believe they were transported); *how the final stones were put into position* (We are still not certain how).

5

Students should already be familiar with the concept of the passive from Unit 1 Lesson 2. This exercise introduces the students to the past simple passive, but indirectly, as they only need to identify and lift parts of the text. You may like to refer to Language Summary 1 on practice page 82. This would also be a good point for students to do Exercises 1 and 2 on that page. Students should do Activity 5 on their own. Check the answers round the class.

Answers

2 *2,300,000 blocks of stone were used.*
3 *After a site for the Great Pyramid was chosen, it was made flat.*
4 *Some people think that the blocks were transported by boat.*
5 *Household goods, clothes, treasure, food and drink were put/placed in the Pyramid.*
6 *The pharaohs' bodies were never discovered in them.*

6

Tell the students to cover the definition while they make suggestions in pairs about what is happening in the picture. Get several suggestions from the class. Did anyone guess correctly?

Answer
In the picture people are burying a time capsule.
After the students have read the definition, ask them if they have ever seen or read about a time capsule. If so, ask them what it contained.
Use the definition together with the picture, and encourage students to talk about time capsules they know about.

7

 Before students answer the specific questions, you could get them to close their books and do some gist listening with the radio broadcast. Check general understanding by giving a few open questions to the class first, eg:
What happened at the school yesterday?
They could then try to answer the questions before hearing the broadcast for the second time. Or you could put the pre-listening questions on the board and tell the class to listen with their books closed.
They can check their answers by reading the gapped text. Next, using the text, students could try to fit the verbs into the gaps before listening again to check the answers. Although there are several possible places to put some of the words, it a useful exercise since the focus is on meaning.
Students would then listen to the text a third time in order to check their answers.

Answers
  2 *was hidden*   3 *was attended*   4 *were put*
  5 *was discovered*   6 *was opened*   7 *were found*

This would be another good point to do Exercises 1 and 2 on practice page 82.

8

This activity provides an opportunity for oral practice of suggestions and reasons, eg: *Let's put a computer in because ...*
Encourage students to defend their suggestions within the group. If necessary give some ways of making suggestions such as, *How about ... , Let's ...* etc.
Group representatives could be chosen to speak to present their five objects and reasons for choosing them. Then students could vote for the time capsule they think is most representative of the time. (You might want to tell them they are not allowed to vote for their own suggestions.)
As a follow-up groups could produce a poster for display with pictures of their time capsule and its contents and the reasons for choosing them.
If students are having difficulty with the choice of *a, an* or *some*, go through Language Summary 2 on practice page 82 at this point, and tell the students to work through Exercise 3.

Homework

Encourage students to think of a suitable headline for the article and write a maximum of 150-200 words describing where and when it was found; who found it; what was inside, and what the public reaction was like.
Encourage students to use the format of the text in Activity 7, and the past simple passive. Enthusiastic students could illustrate their article and present it for display.

Practice *page 82*

Language Summary 1

Refer students back to the texts in Lesson 2 Activities 2 and 7. Ask the students to find examples of the passive in the texts. (As well as the past simple passives there is one passive infinitive, *be disturbed*, but do not make an issue of this.)

1

Students can do Exercise 1 individually or in pairs. Exercises 1 and 2 focus on the form rather than the use of the passive.

Answers
  2 *The site was made flat.*
  3 *(The) stone was cut from a quarry.*
  4 *(The) blocks were moved by the workers.*
  5 *The stones were put in(to) place.*

2

This is a similar exercise and can be done by students on their own and checked in pairs.

Answers
  2 *Money was contributed by the French.*
  3 *In 1885 the stones were taken apart.*
  4 *The stones were transported to New York.*
  5 *The stones were reassembled in New York.*
  6 *The base was made.*
  7 *Finally the statue was dedicated to President Cleveland on October 28th 1886.*

Language Summary 2

Again ask students to pick out examples from Activity 7 before doing the exercise. Emphasize that the choice of *a* or *an* depends upon the sound of the word that follows, not on the noun, eg, *an old bottle*.

3

Students could complete the exercise in pairs.

Answers
  2 *a* 3 *A* 4 *a* 5 *A* 6 *an* 7 *a* 8 *an* 9 *some* 10 *a*
  11 *some* 12 *a*

UNIT 6 LESSON 3

Lesson 3 *The Olympic Games*

Aims: To focus on asking and answering information questions and to stimulate discussion on sport, using a text on the history of the Olympic Games and a radio quiz programme about the Olympics.

Language focus

1 Direct *Wh-* questions
What do you know about the Olympic Games?
When did the Olympic Games start?

2 Indirect *Wh-* questions
Do you know what the word Olympiad means?
Can you tell me how many countries the athletes represent?

Skills focus

- **Reading:** for specific information
- **Listening:** to a radio quiz game for specific information
- **Writing:** quiz questions
- **Speaking:** discussing sport

Vocabulary focus

- Sports: *canoeing, fencing, gymnastics, horse riding, long jump, pistol shooting, running, swimming*

Review

If students have presented their articles (homework for Unit 6 Lesson 2) for display, put them up round the classroom. They can then look at each other's work. You could display the articles with the names hidden, or on the reverse, and encourage the class to make suggestions, which could use the past simple passive, eg:
I think this article was written by Maria Elena, etc.

Warmer

Ask students to bring in pictures (from magazines or posters) of famous athletes from any Olympic sport and organize an identification quiz. This should bring up lots of useful sports vocabulary. Get the students to talk in pairs or groups about their sporting experiences, good and bad, as a spectator and as a participant.
Another possible Warmer activity is to have students cover all the text and see if they can guess what the photograph shows. This could lead to a brief discussion about the flame and the torch bearers.

1

First brainstorm and write on the board what students know about the games. They can then check this against the text. Or students write down five things they want to know about the games, eg:
When did they start? Who pays for them? etc.
Then they read the text to try and find the answers. This activity gives students practice and revision of basic question forms before they practise indirect questions. Monitor and correct the students' accuracy as they write the questions. If they don't find answers to their questions in the text, collate the unanswered questions to see if others know the answers, or set them as homework.

2

Students could do this individually and then correct themselves in groups of four. To make the exercise easier elicit the question forms the students need for each question, eg, a date requires *When?*, a period of time requires *How long?*

Suggested answers

2 *How long are the Olympic Games? How long do the Olympic Games last?*
3 *When were the ancient games ended? When did the ancient games end?*
4 *Who had the idea of organizing a modern Olympic Games?*
5 *What's the Olympic symbol?*
6 *What colours are the rings?*
7 *Where does the Olympic flame traditionally come from?*
8 *Where were the 1992 Olympic games (held)? Where did the 1992 Olympic Games take place?*

3

Encourage students to think of additional differences and get pairs to compare their differences. Finding differences might lead to the question of whether changes are good, or whether comparisons between old and new are not valid. You could make this a competition with students working in pairs.

Suggested answers

In the ancient Olympics only men competed, but now there are men and women. The ancient Olympics lasted one day, but now they last two weeks. There used to be one event, but now there are many. They always used to be held in Olympia, but now they are held in a different city each time. Before there was only one games, but now there are summer and winter games.

4

Make this a class competition and set a time limit. Check vocabulary first: *to host the games* = to have/hold the games; the sports in question 5 – use the sketches to help.

5

Reassure students that they will find out the answers, but not until they have heard William trying the questions on a radio

UNIT 6 LESSON 3

quiz show. The purpose of checking William's answers is to check the students' listening comprehension.

▶ Play the cassette twice if necessary, up to just before the quiz master gives the correct answers.

William's answers

1 a
2 No, last.
3 c
4 b
5 Yes.
6 canoeing, running, fencing, horse riding and pistol shooting
7 No, the International Olympic Committee.
8 b
9 Because of the First and Second World Wars.

6

▶ Allow students time to check in pairs before playing the rest of the cassette where the answers and explanations are given. Give time for students to see how well they did compared with William and with each other.

Quiz answers

1 a
2 Yes.
3 c
4 b
5 No, gold-plated.
6 fencing, swimming, shooting, running and horse riding
7 No, the International Olympic Committee.
8 a
9 Because of the World Wars.

William got five questions right: 1, 3, 4, 7, 9.

7

This team quiz is fun and gives students further opportunity to write questions. You might like to refer to practice page 83 and the Language Summary and focus on forming direct and indirect *wh-* questions before you ask students to write their quiz questions. The points to emphasize are: when we use indirect questions, word order, omission of auxiliaries. Students could do Exercise 1 on practice page 83. The vocabulary exercise on the same page would also give them useful words for their quiz.

You might ask students to include indirect questions in the quiz. Some intonation practice may also be necessary.

Homework

A large-scale class quiz may be possible with students writing questions in teams on topics they choose, eg, current affairs, history, etc, and then asking the rest of the class to answer the questions in their teams. The class could produce a joint written quiz to give another class. The homework activity could be done as a follow-up group or pair writing activity in class. Encourage students to vary the question type by stipulating a minimum of three indirect questions. After checking the questions, arrange the teams facing each other. They take it in turn to ask and answer questions with one person in each team keeping score. If the students have done the questions for homework and are working in large teams get them to check each other's questions and choose the best twenty questions from their group. The quiz should provide some intonation practice for asking questions.

Practice *page 83*

Language Summary

You could start by eliciting different *Wh-* question words and what kind of information they refer to, eg, *who* – a person; *what* – a thing; *when* – a time, *where* – a place, etc.

1

Students do the exercise in pairs or groups. They could then roleplay the interview, or one with another sports personality.

Answers

2 How many brothers and sisters have you got?
   Can you tell me how many brothers and sisters you have got?
3 When did you start running? Can you tell me when you started ...?
4 Why did you become an athlete? Can you tell me why you became ...?
5 Who is your hero? Can you tell me who your hero is?
6 When did you win four gold medals? Can you tell me when you won ...?
7 How often do you train? Can you tell me how often you train?
8 What do you do in your free time? Can you tell me what you do ...?

2

You could get the students to work on their own and check the answers by going through the dialogue in pairs.

Suggested answers

2 I have four brothers and sisters.
3 I started running at school.
4 My athletics teacher encouraged me.
5 My hero is Jesse Owens.
6 I won four gold meals in 1984.
7 I train for three hours a day, every day.
8 In my free time I enjoy, fishing, baseball and watching TV.

3

Encourage students to ask about similar vocabulary related to other sports that they play. Note that *football* in the example refers to soccer, not American football.

Answers

sport	place	equipment
tennis	court	racquet
golf	course	club
weightlifting	gym	weights
swimming	pool	goggles
hockey	pitch	stick
boxing	ring	gloves

37

Unit 7 Collectors' items

The theme of the unit is collecting; things from planes; opinions in market-research surveys; and people, in an extract from a novel.

Lesson 1 *An unusual collection*

Aims: To give students practice in talking about collections and talking about and listening to travel experiences.

Language focus

1 The present perfect and past simple
She's collected over 100 items.
She started her collection five years ago.

2 *Already, yet* and *just*
I've already collected over 100 things.
We have not received permission to land yet.
We have just landed at Loja airport.

Skills focus

- **Speaking:** talking about collections and travel experiences
- **Listening:** to a personal account for specific information
- **Reading:** a magazine article for specific information

Vocabulary focus

- Travel: *airline, pilot, take off, land, runway, oxygen mask, turbulence, flight, luggage*
- Miscellaneous objects: *shoe horn, comb, egg cup, poster, toothbrush, luggage label*

Review

Students present their quizzes. You could have a competition to see which group gains the most marks. You could give extra marks for correct English in questions and answers. Alternatively, display the quizzes and ask students to see how many they can complete in a given time.

Warmer

Ask if any students collect, (or know anyone who collects) or have collected anything in the past. Find out what. If you collect anything, tell the class about it.

1

Students work in pairs. They guess the items collected and talk about their feelings. Check answers round the class and ask some students to say if they already collect or would like to collect the things. Find out which is the most popular or most collected item.

The money for a collection could be a group activity where all members have to agree on something to collect. Or it could be individual and students then mingle and find another student who wants to collect the same thing.
Finish by having pairs or groups report back to the class.

Answers
1 *model planes*   2 *bottles*   3 *insects*   4 *stamps*

2

This is another warmer activity for this particular lesson. Again get students to work in pairs.

Answers
Japan – 1   The Netherlands – 3
Spain – 5   Venezuela – 2

3

Students work alone or in pairs. They may use a dictionary.
Play the cassette once while students tick the items individually. Then let them compare answers in pairs.

Answers
comb – g	knife – h	luggage label – f	pilot's hat – e
poster – l	scarf – b	shoe horn – k	spoon – i
sugar – j	toothbrush – d	toothpaste – c	

Sandra has knives, luggage labels, posters, a scarf, a shoe horn, spoons, sugar and toothpaste.

4

Students read the statements before they listen to the cassette again. Then they compare answers in pairs. Ask them to correct the false statements. After the listening encourage comment: does the collection sound interesting? Would the students be prepared to give over some of their house/flat to such a collection?

Answers
2 *true*
3 *false: She hates it and gets paranoid when she flies.*
4 *false: four years ago*
5 *false: a Lufthansa scarf*
6 *false: from a pilot*
7 *false: in her spare bedroom*
8 *true*
Sandra would now like a pilot's hat or piece of uniform, but she is unlikely to get it.

5

Ask students in pairs to write down possible reasons. Make sure they do not look at the text while they make their suggestions.
They then read the article and check their predictions.

UNIT 7 LESSON 1

6

Students complete the sentences on their own, then compare answers in pairs. Elicit answers from the students and write them up on the board. You could exploit this further by getting students to close their books, and elicit the whole story from the class. Or get the students to work in pairs. Student A has their book closed and tries to retell the main parts of the story. Student B has the book open and corrects/prompts when necessary. They then change roles.

Answers
1 *Sandra felt sick because there was a lot of turbulence.*
2 *Because the pilot didn't have landing permission, they circled the airport for over an hour/the landing was delayed.*
3 *After circling the airport for an hour, the pilot tried to land the plane.*
4 *Some of the oxygen masks came down because they/the plane hit the ground so/very hard.*
5 *When the plane landed, Sandra screamed.*

7

This would be a good time to do Exercise 3 on practice page 84. For the discussion activity get students to close their eyes and recall their worst travel experience for a minute or two before recounting it. Groups could decide what is the worst experience in their group, and one person reports back to the class. Concentrate on the amusing aspects of these stories, but be careful if you think that anyone has had a seriously bad experience or accident that they do not want to talk about.

Homework

As preparation, you could revise letter layout (Unit 1, Lesson 3) on the board. The experience does not have to be bad – it could be an exciting or amusing story. If students make notes on their discussion in Activity 7, this would be helpful for the homework activity. Students who cannot think of a story pretend to be Sandra and write a letter about her bad flight. Follow up: Ask students in pairs to roleplay an interview with Sandra about her flight to Loja. Or get students in pairs to invent a short local news broadcast about a travel disaster, which they could read out and/or record.

Practice *page 84*

Language Summary 1 and 2

Ask students to identify the examples of the present perfect and past simple from the reading and listening texts in the lesson (Activities 3, 4 and 5). Draw the time line for the past simple and *ago* on the board, and elicit real examples from the students, eg: *I left school five years ago.*
Also elicit real examples using the present perfect and *just, yet* and *already*.

1

Tell the students to read the whole letter before they complete the exercise, as tense often depends on the whole context.

Answers
2 *have just flown*   3 *Have you collected*
4 *have flown*   5 *went*
6 *thought*   7 *got*

2

Students do this exercise alone or in pairs. If they ask, point out that *yet* can go in mid-position and *already* can go in end position to give slightly different emphasis:
1 *Sandra has collected over 100 things from aeroplanes already.*
3 *Sandra has not yet got anything from Singapore Airlines.*

Answers
2 *Sandra has just written to Denise.*
3 *Sandra has not got anything from Singapore Airlines yet.*
4 *Denise has already given Sandra lots of things.*
5 *Sandra has not collected her air ticket yet.*
6 *Denise and Rod have just been on holiday to Malta.*

3

Let the students read the whole text first, and answer vocabulary queries, if necessary. *Queue* = a line of people waiting; *customs official* = the person who checks you aren't bringing in/taking out anything illegal; *gate* = the place where you get on a particular plane.
Students do the exercise alone, then compare answers in pairs.
Extend the activity by brainstorming travel vocabulary on the board, under the headings of *bus, train, boat, car*.

Answers
2 *check-in*   3 *luggage*   4 *ticket*
5 *passport*   6 *departure lounge* 7 *duty free*
8 *flight*   9 *plane*   10 *took off*

4

Either do this as a whole class activity or competition, or let students work in pairs. They should try the exercise without dictionaries at first.

Answers
2 *wear – whe(r)e*
3 *wa(l)k – fork*
4 *(k)now – go*
5 *w(h)y – die*
6 *com(b) – home*
7 *brou(gh)t – port*
8 *ni(gh)t – white*

UNIT 7 LESSON 2

Lesson 2 *Collecting information*

Aim: To give students practice in conducting and writing up a class survey.

Language focus

1 Present perfect simple and present perfect continuous
How much TV have you watched this week?
I've been watching more than usual this week.

2 Polite requests
Could you spare a couple of minutes?
May I just ask a few questions?
Would you mind answering a few questions?

Skills focus

- **Listening:** for main ideas in market research interviews, and identifying key vocabulary
- **Writing:** questions for a survey, taking notes and writing up the results
- **Speaking:** asking questions for information

Vocabulary focus

- Air travel: *tourist, business, first class, cabin crew*
- TV: *viewing, comedy show, detective series*
- Collecting: *auction, antique shop, unusual*

Review

Ask several students to tell you and the class about their journey to class today.

1

The class should speculate about the photo in pairs or groups. Then ask some of the students to share their ideas with the whole class. The topic of market research should come up. If not, introduce it and brainstorm topics for market research. Also elicit reasons for carrying out such research. If any students have been interviewed for research, ask them to tell the class about it.

2

▣ Play the four interviews once without pausing. Students write down the topics in order. Then let them compare their answers in pairs. You may want to confirm the topics before the students listen for key vocabulary. (See the table in the next column for the answers.)
▣ Play the cassette again and let students write down the key vocabulary for each topic. They then compare their answers in

pairs again. Elicit the answers, and write them up on the board.
Extend the activity by brainstorming other topic-related vocabulary for each list.

Answers

	topic	key words
2	television	viewing (habits), watch, TV, programmes, comedy shows, detective series
3	hobbies	leisure, interests, free time, cinema, film, football, collecting bottles, weekends
4	airline services	passenger service, flight, first/business/tourist class, company, food, cabin crew, seats

3

Jacob was the young man interviewed in the third interview. See what students can remember about him before they look at the notes. Point out that more than one word is sometimes needed to fill in the gaps.
Ask the students to complete the exercise alone or in pairs. Check the answers with the class.

Answers
2 *22*
4 *collecting bottles*
5 *when*
6 *gave him a ship in a bottle for a birthday present*
7 *over 300 bottles (in his collection)*
8 *a bottle in bluish glass in the shape of a fish*

This would be a suitable time to look at Language Summary 1 on practice page 85. Students can do Exercises 1 and 2.

4

Refer students back to the market research topics they brainstormed in Activity 1 for ideas if necessary. Arrange students in groups of four. Give them ten to fifteen minutes to write the questions. Monitor the groups, helping students to correct their questions. Make sure all the students in each group have the questions written down and space to write the answers.

5

Elicit polite request forms from the interviews and drill pronunciation if necessary. This would be a good point to go through Language Summary 2 on practice page 85, and for the students to do Exercise 3 on the same page.
Encourage students to use polite requests when conducting their surveys. Let them mingle and interview any four other students in the class. Ensure that they write notes, not full sentences when interviewing. Give ten to fifteen minutes for students to conduct their interviews.
Students return to their original groups and compare their

UNIT 7 LESSON 2

answers. Each group appoints a group spokesperson to report any interesting findings to the rest of the class. For example, if interviewing on travel:
Ten people have visited another country.
Four people have been to Finland.
If a number of students have chosen the same topic, they could combine their findings to make a fuller survey or a class display.
Follow-up: In place of, or as well as, the general class survey, conduct a market research survey on products. Each group chooses a product, for example, washing powder, magazines, etc. Students bring in three or four different makes of the same product and write questions to find out which make people prefer and why. They could write questions about the packet, size, price, quality, availability, etc.
Or, following on from the above survey and/or Activity 5, get the students to write up the results of their surveys. First make sure they know phrases like: *the majority/most people thought that/preferred ...* or *seven out of ten people preferred ...*

Homework

Tell students to use the text in Activity 3 as a model. Remind them to pay attention to the tenses they use, particularly the present perfect and past simple.

Practice *page 85*

Language Summary 1

Before students do the exercise, you could get them to listen to the interview extracts from Lesson 2 again and identify the examples of the present perfect simple and continuous that they hear. Use these examples to illustrate the grammar explanation.

1

Students do the exercise alone or in pairs. Check the answers round the class.

Answers
2 *Jacob has been collecting bottles for ten years.*
3 *Jacob and Tim have been sharing a flat for two years.*
4 *Jacob has been studying hard this month.*
5 *Jacob and Tim have been arguing a lot recently.*
6 *Jacob has been going out with Elena for two months.*
7 *Tim has been feeling ill all weekend.*

2

Tell students to read the whole text first and perhaps answer a few questions to check general comprehension. For example:
What does Janet do?

Does she like her job?
Why/ why not?
Then get students to complete the exercise alone or in pairs.

Answers
1 *has been*
2 *has interviewed*
3 *has found out*
4 *has been studying*
5 *has been doing*
6 *have had*
7 *has been*
8 *have been getting up*
9 *have been applying for*

Language Summary 2

Refer students back to the polite request forms they used in Lesson 2 Activity 5. Write them on the board. If appropriate, explain how *could* and *may* are replaced by *can* in more informal situations.

3

Students complete the requests on their own.
Extend the activity by eliciting possible positive and negative responses to requests. Examples: *Certainly. Of course* or *I'm sorry, I'm busy at the moment.*
Drill requests and responses if necessary. Students then mingle and make five different requests to five other students, eg:
Could I borrow your pencil please?
May I open the window?
Would you mind closing the door?
Students have to comply with the request or give an excuse.

Answers
2 *May/Could I borrow your pen?*
3 *Could you help me with this survey?*
4 *Would you mind filling in this questionnaire?*
5 *Would you mind helping us with our survey?*
6 *May/Could I ask you a few questions about your work?*
7 *Could you answer a few questions?*
8 *Would you mind giving us your opinion of this product?*
9 *Could you say which you prefer?*
10 *Could you spare a few minutes?*

4

Students do this exercise alone or in pairs. For some questions there are several possibilities, although there is only one combination that allocates two nouns for each verb. Point out that *to go for a drink* = to go to a bar/pub, not to a cafe for a cup of tea.

Answers
1 *to watch TV/the news*   2 *to listen to the radio/a concert*
3 *to have dinner/a picnic*   4 *to go for a walk/for a drink*
5 *to play football/the piano*   6 *to spend time/money*

UNIT 7 LESSON 3

Lesson 3 'The Collector'

Aim: To give students practice in understanding an unsimplified extract from a novel.

Language focus

-ing form
Then she was right beside me, coming up the pavement.
They passed talking nineteen to the dozen.

Skills focus

- **Reading:** a narrative taken from a novel for main ideas and vocabulary prediction
- **Speaking:** role-playing a police interview
- **Listening:** to a news report for specific information

Vocabulary focus

- Ways of looking: *to watch, to see, to flash a look, to peer/look in*
- Movement: *to bend down, to pass, to get out, to run over, to dash out, to stand back*

The Collector is a 20th century novel written by John Fowles, a British novelist. The first half tells the story from Frederick's point of view, the second half tells the same story, but from Miranda's point of view in the form of diary entries. It was made into a film.

Review and Warmer

Conduct a short class survey on reading habits, eg:
What kinds of books do students read? Do they read magazines or newspapers? How often do they read for pleasure? Do they read in English for pleasure?

1

Ask students to suggest adjectives that describe Frederick as he appears in the picture. They can work in pairs or alone, or you could make this a class activity and brainstorm ideas, writing them on the board.

2

Students work in groups of three or four. Give them two to three minutes to decide what Frederick will do, and ask a person for each group to share the group's ideas with the whole class. Ensure they don't look at the text yet.
Encourage the students to read quickly for the main ideas and not to worry about the gaps or words they don't understand. They should guess meaning in context and underline a maximum of five words or phrases they don't understand, which can be discussed afterwards. Vocabulary students may ask about includes: *overcast* = a sky with a lot of low dark clouds; *spot with rain* = rain a little; *talking nineteen to the dozen* = talking very fast; *to dash* = to move suddenly and fast; *to peer in* = to look in cautiously; *to flash a look* = to look quickly.
How close were the students' predictions?
The next two questions are to prompt discussion. You may prefer not to tell them what actually happens if you intend them to invent their own ending later.

Answers
Frederick is telling the story.
Frederick has kidnapped Miranda because he sees her as another beautiful butterfly to keep and admire.
Miranda tries to escape several times and fails. She eventually falls ill. Frederick does not know what to do and so she dies.

3

Ask students to give reasons for their choices when going over their answers, eg: 2 is *umbrellas* because it was raining.

Answers
1 *pass*	**2** *umbrellas*	**3** *no one*
4 *surprised*	**5** *awful*	**6** *move*

4

Tell students to look at the police form first and ask about any unknown vocabulary: *build* = physical shape, eg, fat or thin.
▣ Play the cassette once and let students compare information in pairs. Then play the cassette again.
Elicit the answers in sentences from the students and write them up in note form on the board. Example:
She was wearing a blue jumper and ...

Answers
MISSING PERSON REPORT FORM
Name: *Miranda Grey*
Age: *20*
Address: *Hampstead, North London*
Occupation: *art student*
Description:
Height: *5' 4" (five foot four inches)*
Build: *slim*
Hair: *long, blonde*
Clothes: *blue jumper, white blouse, dark green skirt*
Place of disappearance:
between the cinema and her home
Time: *between about 6 and 8 pm*

5

It may be helpful to divide the class in two for all the students A to prepare together. Students B could do the same, though they will be acting as individuals. Give the police officers a few minutes to think of other questions. The witnesses need to re-read the text in Activity 2 and the completed police report form in Activity 4 to help them remember the details of the events.

UNIT 7 LESSON 3

During the roleplay books should be closed, however, and students should be encouraged to invent anything they forget or don't know. Give them ten to fifteen minutes to do the roleplay. Make sure the police officers take notes during the interview. Also make sure there is enough time for the students to change roles, otherwise half the class will have difficulty with their homework.

Follow-up: Students work in groups of four: one is Frederick, one is Miranda, and the other two are other invented characters. They could write or improvise a script for a scene later in the novel.
Or students write a short newspaper article about Miranda's disappearance. For this they should refer to the news report.
Or students write the next paragraph of the narrative after the kidnapping. They can refer to their ideas in Activity 2.

Homework

The police officers write up their interview, eg:
The witness was walking up ... Road when s/he saw a girl. S/he was returning from work.
If they prefer, the witnesses could write up their own statements, eg:
I was walking up ... Road at about 6.30 pm when ...
You could elicit some possible first sentences from the students and write them on the board to give an idea. Ask students to write about 100 words.

Practice *page 86*

Language Summary 1

You could write on the board the two examples from the text in Lesson 3 Activity 2:
Then she was right behind me, coming up the pavement.
They passed talking nineteen to the dozen.
Ask the students to identify the subject of each of the *-ing* verbs, and which order the events occur in. In the first example *she* is the subject of *coming*, and in the second *they* is the subject of *talking*. In both cases the events are simultaneous.

1

Then ask the students to do the exercise alone or in pairs.

Answers
2 – *a*   3 – *c*   4 – *d*   5 – *e*   6 – *g*   7 – *f*

2

Tell the students to read the whole text first and ask them a few comprehension questions, eg:
Where did she go?
Who/What did she see?
What do you think the object was?
Students do the exercise alone or in pairs.

Answers
2 *singing*   3 *barking*   4 *talking*
5 *Putting on*   6 *lying*   7 *wearing*
8 *Feeling*

3

You could ask students to identify all the verbs of movement in the text in Lesson 3 Activity 2 before doing the exercise. Students could work in pairs, matching the pictures and the verbs and then using each verb in an example sentence, eg:
Marcia lay down for an hour because she didn't feel well.
Or extend the activity by getting students to combine the verbs of movement with another verb in the *-ing* form, eg:
Marcia lay down, feeling ill.

Answers
1 *run*   2 *walk*   3 *bend down*
4 *climb up*   5 *jump*   6 *lie down*
7 *sit down*   8 *stand up*

4

Allow students to use a dictionary for this exercise, if they need to. They should work alone or in pairs.

Answers
2 *looked, saw*   3 *was staring*
4 *saw*   5 *watched, didn't see*
6 *Look*

5

Let students do this exercise in pairs, and then compare answers with another pair. Tell them to underline the differences, then write in the correct words. They can check their answers with the text in Lesson 3 Activity 2.

Answers
1 *men – women*
2 *walking sticks – umbrellas*
3 *snow – spot with rain*
4 *came across – came up*
5 *lay down – bent right down*
6 *laughing – talking (nineteen to the dozen)*
7 *bus – van*
8 *no cars parked anywhere – cars parked everywhere*
9 *Ten minutes – A minute*
10 *closed – opened*

Unit 8 A week of entertainment

This unit is about organizing a festival. The first two lessons are aimed at giving students the necessary language and skills practice to enable them to participate in a festival committee roleplay in the third lesson.

Lesson 1 *What's on?*

Aim: To give students practice in making social arrangements by making and replying to suggestions.

Language focus

1 Making and replying to suggestions
What about going Scottish dancing? I'm sorry, I can't.
How about some spaghetti? OK, fine.
Why don't we watch the fireworks?
Let's go to a club.
Shall we go to the cinema?

2 Stating preferences
I'd prefer to go Scottish dancing.

Skills focus

- **Reading:** a festival programme for specific information, and for interest
- **Speaking:** making social arrangements
- **Listening:** to a conversation for specific language

Vocabulary focus

- Entertainment: *an exhibition, fireworks, mime, a play, a fashion show, a talk, batik, a slide show*
- Adjectives of opinion: *amazing, spectacular, entertaining, fascinating, dramatic, unforgettable, unusual, awful, disappointing*

Review

Students get into two teams. One team thinks of someone in the class. A member of the other team asks a member of the first team questions about the person's appearance, and tries to guess who it is. Award points for guessing correctly, and for correct questions.

Warmer

Students write down three activities on a piece of paper: something they like doing for a 'night out'; something to do at a weekend; something they find really boring. They then discuss each other's activities.
Or students discuss in pairs what entertainment they have planned for the coming weekend, or what they did the previous weekend.

1
Encourage the students to guess what is going on if they don't know. If you have students from different countries, find out and discuss the traditional activities from their countries.

Answers
1 *Batik dying from Indonesia.*
2 *Ballet from France.*
3 *Tai Chi from China.*

2
Tell the students not to worry about reading and understanding all the words in the text, but to skim it for words and phrases that indicate which event is being advertised in each case. Set a time limit of a few minutes to encourage reading quickly for the main idea. Students do this exercise alone and then compare answers in pairs. Or check answers round the class.

Answers
a dinner, fireworks, a talk

3
Play the cassette once and allow the students to discuss it in pairs. Play it again if necessary. Allow further discussion before eliciting the answers.

Answers
They agree to go to the dinner on Sunday, to the Moscow acrobats on Thursday, and to the fireworks display and the Samba band on Saturday.

4
Pause the cassette between the extracts to allow time for students to discuss in pairs, and then write in the words. Ask students to identify the phrases which make suggestions, reply to suggestions, and state a preference. Write them up on the board and elicit other possible answers. Examples:
How about playing tennis?
How about going for a drink?
Give help with pronunciation and intonation, and drill if necessary so that students can use the phrases in Activity 6.

Answers
Geoff: OK, fine.
2 *Geoff: And let's go ...*
Suzie: I'd prefer to go ... How about that?
Brian: Yeah, great idea.
Geoff: I'm sorry, I can't.
3 *Geoff: And ... er ... shall we go to the cinema ...*
Suzie: Well, I'd prefer to do ...
Geoff: Well, what about ...

This would be a good time to go through the Language Summary on practice page 87, and for students to do Exercise 1 on that page.

44

UNIT 8 LESSON 1

5

Give the class about 15 minutes for this exercise, and ask each group to choose a spokesperson to report back to the class which events their group is going to and how much it will cost in total.

Go round the groups, monitoring and helping where necessary. Make a note of any general language problems and give additional practice afterwards. If making suggestions is causing problems, students could do Exercise 2 on practice page 87. If they found the vocabulary difficult when they first read the programme, let them do Exercise 3 on practice page 87 before they start the group activity.

6

Tell the students to work alone. Then they check their answers in pairs. Help with vocabulary, or allow the use of dictionaries as necessary.

Answers
1 S/he enjoyed the mime. Key words: *incredible energy and skill, entertaining, enjoyed.*
2 S/he didn't enjoy the fun run. Key words: *cold, awful, too long, disappointing.*

As a follow-up, ask students to watch a TV programme on a particular day, and review it without mentioning the actual name. The reviews are posted round the classroom wall, and students in pairs go round and try to identify which programme was reviewed and whether the review was positive or negative. This could also be used as a Review activity for Unit 8 Lesson 2.

Homework

In preparation brainstorm and write on the board possible positive and negative adjectives of opinion from the lesson and as suggested by the students. Give help with pronunciation. Also elicit a list of possible aspects of an event to review/comment on, such as performer, location, cost, comfort, quality, organization, interest, etc. Students should write about 50-60 words. They may like to follow the pattern of one of the reviews in Activity 6.

Practice *page 87*

Language Summary

Ask students to close their books and see how many of the phrases for making and replying to suggestions they can remember from Lesson 1. Go through the Language Summary if necessary.

1

Students then do the exercise alone or in pairs. Extend the activity by getting them to make up similar dialogues.

Answers
1 *don't you come*   2 *about going*   3 *we try*
4 *don't we go*   5 *'s meet*   6 *we meet*
7 *about going*   8 *don't we go*

2

Students work individually, and use any of the suggestion forms they have met to make suggestions. You may want to insist they give reasons for refusing suggestions.
Extend the activity to a whole class activity. Ask students to make suggestions orally to five other students and to reply to any suggestions made to them.

Answers
2 *Why don't we/Let's/Shall we go to the beach this/next/at the weekend?*
   How/What about going to the beach this/next/at the weekend?
3 *Why don't we/Let's/Shall we go cycling/for a bike ride this afternoon?*
   How/What about going cycling/for a bike ride this afternoon?
4 *Why don't we/Let's/Shall we have a cup of tea now?*
   How/What about (having) a cup of tea now?
5 *Why don't we/Let's/Shall we have spaghetti tomorrow?*
   How/What about eating spaghetti tomorrow?
6 *Why don't we/Let's/Shall we play football on Thursday?*
   How/What about playing football on Thursday?
7 *Why don't we/Let's/Shall we go dancing on Friday?*
   How/What about going dancing on Friday?
8 *Why don't we/Let's/Shall we go to Paris next summer?*
   How/What about going to Paris next summer?

3

Students do this exercise alone or in pairs. Let them use a dictionary if they need to. Write up the answers on the board under the three columns and give help with pronunciation. Extend the activity by getting students to provide other words they know related to the topics. They then fill in the gaps.

Answers

Theatre	Music	Sport
actor	audience	marathon
audience	band	play (verb)
box office	box office	player
play (noun)	concert	referee
ticket	play (verb)	player
	singer	spectator
		ticket

2 *band*   3 *music*   4 *audience*   5 *play*
6 *actor*   7 *box office*   8 *tickets*

45

UNIT 8 LESSON 2

Lesson 2 *A celebrity guest*

Aims: To give students practice in listening to a formal talk, and to write a publicity article for a festival brochure.

Language focus

1 Non-defining relative clauses
This is me on top of Mount Hekla, which last erupted in 1981.
First he went to Timbuktu, where he bought two camels.

2 Phrasal verbs
Then he set out on his epic journey.
He soon ran into problems.

Skills focus

- **Listening:** to a formal talk for the main idea and for detail
- **Writing:** a publicity article
- **Reading:** a publicity article

Vocabulary focus

- Geographical features: *desert, sand, glacier, volcano*
- Miscellaneous: *camel, scorpion, to sting, bones, to suffer*

Review

Display the reviews the students wrote for their homework (Unit 8, Lesson 1) around the classroom. Group reviews of the same item together, and note how many positive and negative reviews each item has.

Warmer

Brainstorm what students associate with the desert, and discuss what difficulties there might be living in the desert. Or get students to write down the name of a celebrity guest they would like to invite to give a talk at a festival, and write down one question they would ask the guest. Students then discuss their choices in groups.
See how much students can remember about Ted Edwards from the programme in Lesson 1 Activity 2. Then look at the photo of Ted and let students decide what kind of a man he is.

1

Students speculate in pairs about the numbers. Tell them not to look at the passage at this stage.
They then do the activity. Answer vocabulary queries after they have done it. If students ask: 5 *miles* = 8 kilometres; *self-sufficient* = without help; *to sting* = to bite, or to injure with a sting (insects); *to run out of* = to have no more.

Answers
1 *1983*
2 *nineteen-day*
3 *350*
4 *two*
5 *45°*
6 *25 kilograms*

2

Students discuss the answers in pairs. They should scan the text for the key words to give the information.

Answers
Ted was a school drama teacher.
It was the longest self-sufficient solo journey in history.
He fell off a camel.
A BBC (British Broadcasting Corporation) television crew met him.
You may want to look at Language Summary 1 on practice page 88 at this point. The students could do Exercise 2.

3

If the phrasal verbs in the reading passage caused problems, you could go through Language Summary 2 on practice page 88 at this point, and let the students do Exercise 3.
Ask students to describe the photos to elicit vocabulary they will need for the listening exercise. Examples: *glacier, volcano, waterfall, to climb, to be/get lost, a map*. (See the tapescript for other words they may need.)
Students work in pairs and predict where Ted went and what he saw. Then they compare predictions with another pair.
▶ Play the cassette through once.

Answers
From left to right:
2 – the volcano
4 – the end of his journey
3 – the river
1 – the glacier

4

▶ Students could work in pairs or groups for this activity. Play the cassette twice, if necessary. Ask students to give their answers in full sentences from their notes, eg:
Ted went from Seydisfjordur to Reykjavik.

Answers

Where Ted went	from Seydisfjordur to Reykjavik (in Iceland)
When he went	in summer (June-July) 1984
Length of journey	24 days, about 800 kilometres or 510 miles
What he did	climbed on a glacier; climbed up a volcano; crossed rivers; crossed a volcanic desert
Who he met	no one
Problems he had	fell climbing the glacier; burnt himself on the volcano; got lost; got hungry; got very cold

After students have discussed their ideas with their partner, the pairs can form groups of four and continue the discussion. Remind them to give reasons for their views. Have some groups report back to the class, and end by seeing if you can reach class agreement.

This would be a good point to consolidate practice of non-defining relative clauses. The students could do Exercise 1 on practice page 88 here.

Follow-up: In pairs, students roleplay an interview with the Camel Man, about his life. One student is the journalist, the other is Ted.

5

Remind students that the aim of the article is to promote the talk for the festival, that is, to persuade people to attend it, so that the article must make the expedition sound exciting. Use the reading text in Activity 1 as a model. Students should only make notes in class.

Homework

Tell students to write no more than 100 words. Students might like to present the article in an interesting way, with illustrations and perhaps a simple map.

Practice *page 88*

1

Ask students to keep their books closed and see how much information they can remember about Ted Edwards before they do the exercise. If necessary, go through Language Summary 1 first.

Answers
1 *who* 2 *which* 3 *who* 4 *where* 5 *which* 6 *which*
7 *where* 8 *who*

2

See if students can make up any more non-defining relative clauses about any of the people or places. Example:
In 1984 Ted went to Iceland, which is a volcanic island/where he walked from coast to coast/which lies near the Arctic Circle.
They can do the exercise on their own, and compare answers with their partner, or check them round the class.

Answers
2 *which is an island in the Atlantic Ocean.*
3 *where he burnt his leg.*
4 *which is the largest glacier in Europe.*
5 *where there are no plants, animals or people.*
6 *who are journalists.*

3

Students may need to do this exercise, and go through the Language Summary, before they do the reading activities in Lesson 2.

Answers
2 *stopped*
3 *hope to enjoy*
4 *arrived (unexpectedly)*
5 *started a journey*

4

This is a fun activity to be done in pairs or groups. You could make it into a competition, and see who can complete it first. Take marks off for errors.

Answers
1 *FESTIVAL ALREADY*
2 *ACTOR ORGANIZE*
3 *THEATRE RESTAURANT*
4 *PROGRAMME MEAL*
5 *CINEMA MANAGER*
6 *MIME MENU*
7 *MUSICAL ALWAYS*
8 *OPERA RAN*
9 *DISCO CONCERT*

UNIT 8 LESSON 3

Lesson 3 *Choosing a programme*

Aims: To give students practice in running a committee meeting, and planning a festival programme.

Language focus

1 Expressing agreement and disagreement
I think it's too difficult to get costumes. – So do I.
I don't think this is a good idea. – Neither do I.
I don't think the town hall's too small. – Well I do.

2 Talking about likes and dislikes
You know people enjoy watching good films.
You don't like the idea of a pop group.

Skills focus

- **Speaking:** roleplaying a committee meeting and deciding on a programme
- **Writing:** a festival programme
- **Listening:** to a committee meeting for specific information and taking notes

Vocabulary focus

- Entertainment: *karaoke, venue, mask, magician, football pitch, fancy-dress*

If students get really involved in the roleplay, the activities in this lesson may take two lessons.

Review

Students present their articles (homework for Unit 8 Lesson 2) to the class. Or display them round the room. Each student then votes to go or not to go to the talk, on the basis of the articles. See how many decide to go. Try to find which was the most persuasive article, and why.

1

This is a warmer activity that should provide groups with suggestions for possible festival activities for the roleplay. Extend the activity by getting students to think of other suggestions for festival activities and write them on the board.

Answers
The items in the picture are: a wine bottle and glass, a tennis racket and ball, a drum, a paint brush and a pot of paint, a parachute, a rabbit in a hat.

2

Give the students a few minutes to make their own choices, filling in the first column of the table. Explain any necessary vocabulary.
Go round monitoring as they discuss their choices with a partner. Remind them to use the language of suggestions and reasons.
▶ Play all the cassette section once. The students mark the middle column as they listen.
They can then check their answers in pairs. (See the answers in the completed table below.)

3

▶ If necessary, pause the cassette in the middle of the second playing to give students time to write notes. Play it a third time if necessary.

Answers

	The committee's choice	Reasons
a jazz group	✓	really popular
5-a-side football	✗	nowhere to play, no decent pitch
Greek folk group	✓	something different, spectacular
children's art exhibition	✓	get children involved, parents will like it
lecture/slide show on Everest	?	no news yet
fancy-dress disco	✗	too difficult to get costumes, too much time to make a fancy-dress
celebrity golf match	?	

Make sure the students give reasons for their own choices, and opinions on the committee's decisions. You may want to go through Language Summary 1 on practice page 89 at this point, and let the students do Exercise 1.

4

Write up the original sentences on the board while the students do the matching exercise. Then write up the answers underneath the similar sentences as you elicit them from the students. Practise pronunciation and intonation. Erase the sentences, leaving just the functions on the board, and see how many of the phrases the students can remember. Extend the activity by inviting students to suggest other phrases with a similar meaning.

Answers
2 – c   3 – e   4 – a   5 – b

UNIT 8 LESSON 3

5
Put students into groups of four. Tell groups to choose a committee secretary to write down the decisions taken. It does not have to be the chairperson. If your class does not divide into groups of four, some groups could have a fifth person who is the secretary.
It would be a good idea to do practice page 89 Exercises 1, 2 and 3 before the students do the roleplay. You may need to go through both the Language Summaries with the class. There should be enough information on page 53 of the Student's Book for the class to perform the roleplay successfully. However, you will need to monitor carefully and give help and encouragement where necessary. Students may or may not want to prepare in role groups as they usually do for a roleplay. There is a lot to get through, so keep an eye on time.

6 and Homework
Students will need their notes for this part of the activity. Remind them of the importance of clear, accurate English. Encourage them to present the programme in such a way that people will really want to come to the festival. If possible, make arrangements for another class learning English at a similar level to visit the classroom display once it is completed.

Practice *page 89*

Language Summary 1
Write up on the board a few opinions from the committee meeting in Lesson 3 Activity 2. For example:
I think a pop group's too expensive.
I think it's too difficult to get a costume for fancy-dress.
I think a jazz group is a great idea.
Next elicit expressions of agreement and disagreement from the whole class.

1
Students then do the exercise, alone or in pairs.
Extend the activity by getting students in pairs to do a similar exercise orally. Student A voices an opinion on an aspect of entertainment, for example:
I really like disco music.
or *I enjoy yoga classes.*
Student B has to reply according to their opinion. Then they swap roles. They continue for five or six opinions each.
Point out that *not keen on* and *not fond of* can be used positively without *not* and that like the other verbs in the dialogue they are followed by *-ing*.

Extend this with a class mingle activity. Students have to talk to six other students and express a violent like or dislike. For example:
I hate playing football.
The other students have to respond. Use this as sentence stress/intonation practice.

Answers

Positive	Neutral	Negative
love	don't mind	don't really like
enjoy		can't stand
really like		not very keen on
		not very fond of

2
You will probably need to go through Language Summary 2 with the class before they do Exercise 2. You may want them to pick out expressions of agreement and disagreement from Lesson 3.
Students can do the exercise on their own. They check the answers in pairs, reading them out as a dialogue, and taking turns to give the original statement and the reaction.

Answers
2 *Oh, I don't.*
3 *Nor/neither do I.*
4 *So do I/Me too.*
5 *Oh, I don't.*
6 *So do I/Me too.*
7 *So do I/Me too.*
8 *Oh, I do.*

3
After correcting the exercise ask students to practise the intonation. You may want to do some choral drilling.

Answers
1 – D   2 – A   3 – A   4 – A   5 – D   6 – A

4
Let the students go through the texts again if they want to. They can work alone and check their answers in pairs. You could use the stress exercise as a class drill.

Answers
awful – N   entertaining – P   popular – P
boring – N   excellent – P   spectacular – P
disappointing – N   exciting – P   unusual – P
                interesting – P

Unit 9 The natural world

The theme of this unit is the natural environment, focusing on whales and other animals, and on climatic conditions such as typhoons, sandstorms, etc.

Lesson 1 Whales

Aims: To give students practice in talking about whales and comparing them with other animals and humans.

Language focus

1 Comparatives with *as ... as*
The Blue Whale can weigh as much as 150 tonnes.
The situation isn't as bad as that.

2 Revision of comparatives and superlatives
It is larger than any other animal; in fact it is the largest animal that has ever lived.

3 Revision of present perfect
Whales have existed for over 70,000 years.

Skills focus

- **Reading:** a factual text for main ideas and detail
- **Listening:** to a radio discussion for main ideas and people's opinions
- **Speaking:** explaining opinions to someone who disagrees with them

Vocabulary focus

- Whale products: *lipstick, face cream, paint, perfume, detergent, candle*
- Environmental terms: *environment, extinction, livelihood, feeding habits, breed, plankton*
- Adjectives of description: *gentle, remarkable, developed, sophisticated, intelligent*

Review

Display all the festival brochures round the classroom. If possible, invite another class to look at the display and say which events they would like to attend. Otherwise ask the class to do the same thing. They can also vote for the best-produced brochure.

Warmer

Write up a list of animals on the board (suggested list: *whale, alligator, frog, horse, eagle, bat, shark, dog, spider, bee, rat, cat, rabbit, lion, snake*) and ask students to work in groups to categorize them in any way they like, eg:
mammals, reptiles etc; dangerous and non-dangerous; those that can fly or swim and those that can't; numbers of legs, etc. Groups report back to the whole class.

1

Students work on their own to write down their three facts about whales. If the class find this very difficult, start by brainstorming a few ideas and putting them on the board. They then compare ideas with two other students. They may change their minds if they wish to.
Tell the students to keep their lists to see if the information in the reading text confirms their facts.

2

Students do this activity alone. They then compare their answers in pairs. They could use a dictionary.

Answers
2 – b   3 – j   4 – a   5 – d   6 – f   7 – h   8 – i   9 – e   10 – g
All of these products could have parts made from whales, and all have been made from whales in the past, although this is no longer the case.

3

You may need to help students understand statements 2 and 4 if they are not familiar with the pattern *as ... as*. Perhaps look at Language Summary 1 on practice page 90, and get the students to do Exercise 1 on that page first.
Make sure the pairs guess the answers before they look at the text.
Remind the class that they do not need to understand every word, but that they should scan the text for key words to find the answers to the questions.
Once students have done the true/false activity tell them to check their three facts from Activity 1. They can discuss their reactions to the facts in pairs, or you could have a short class discussion.

Answers
1 F – over 70,000   2 T
3 F – over 30 m   4 F – it is the largest animal that has ever lived
5 F – up to an hour   6 T
7 T

4

First check that students understand all the topics. They should again scan the paragraphs for key words.

Answers
breathing – 3
communication – 3
feeding habits – 4
length of time in existence – 1
navigation – 3
playing – 4
types of whales – 1

5

The photo is from a Greenpeace anti-whaling brochure.

Greenpeace is an international environmental pressure group. Discuss the photo in pairs or as a whole class. Pairs should report back to the class.

6

Make sure students understand what a radio phone-in is, and get suggestions as to what sort of topics are discussed. This phone-in is quite fast with some difficult vocabulary so tell the students not to worry about understanding every word. They only need to pick out who is for, and who is against whaling, ie, they are listening for gist.

 Play the cassette once.

Answers
The woman supports whaling; the man is against whaling.
Give students time to read the statements and ask about vocabulary, eg: *close to extinction* = about to die out; *source of meat* = providing meat; *livelihood* = means of living; *a ban on something* = something is illegal or forbidden; *to depend on something* = something is necessary or essential.
 Play the cassette again for students to mark the reasons they hear.

Answers
3 – B   5 – A   7 – B   9 – A   10 – B

Once you have checked the answers, give time for the students to decide what they feel, and discuss their opinions in pairs. If they make notes on their discussion, this would be helpful for their homework.

Homework

Formal letter layout and conventions are dealt with fully in Unit 10, Lesson 3. The main idea here is for students to express their opinions. Remind them to give reasons.

Practice *page 90*

1

You could elicit some *as ... as* comparisons between whales and humans and write them on the board to get students started. Then they do the exercise alone or in pairs. Note that we usually understand not *as ... as* to mean *less ... than*, eg: *not as old as* = younger than; *not as long as* = shorter than.

Answers
2 *The lion's tail is as long as the tiger's.*
3 *The lion is as heavy as the tiger./The lion weighs as much as the tiger.*
4 *The tiger's jump is not as long as the lion's./The tiger can't jump as far as the lion.*
5 *The lion isn't as good at swimming as the tiger./The lion can't swim as well as the tiger.*
6 *The lion has the same number of cubs as the tiger./The lion has as many cubs as the tiger.*
7 *The tiger cubs don't spend as much time/as long with their parents as lion cubs.*

Students work alone or in pairs to write three more sentences. Ask some of them to report back to the class.

Language Summary 2

Revise the rules for comparatives and superlatives by eliciting example sentences from the whales text in Lesson 1 Activity 3 and writing them up under the two headings. Next ask students to make up more comparatives and superlatives either using the lion/tiger information from Exercise 1, or from their own knowledge. Then ask students to explain the rules for comparatives and superlatives before doing the exercise.

2

Students can do the exercise on their own and check answers in pairs as a dialogue.

Answers
2 *the ugliest*   3 *as bad as*
4 *the largest*   5 *the largest*
6 *wide as*   7 *bigger*
8 *the most dangerous* 9 *the most interesting*
10 *fast as*   11 *better*

3

Tell students to read the whole text first for meaning.

Answers
2 *have ever attacked*
3 *have also attacked*
4 *has caused*
5 *have recorded*
6 *has ever lived*
7 *have seen*
8 *have existed*
9 *have always hunted*

UNIT 9 LESSON 2

Lesson 2 *Favourite animals*

Aims: To give students practice in describing different animals and reporting what other people have said.

Language focus

1 Reported speech
Police said the tenant was a civilian.
Reinstaedt told reporters that there was a python in the hall.

2 *say* and *tell*
They said that they thought he was currently on holiday.
Police told reporters that US authorities were helping to locate him.

Skills focus

- **Listening:** to descriptions of animals
- **Writing:** descriptions of animals
- **Reading:** a newspaper article for main ideas

Vocabulary focus

- Animals: *python, crocodile, lizard, bull, fox, rat, mouse, rabbit, eagle, snake, penguin, zebra, donkey, elephant*
- Animal parts of the body: *fur, horns, tail, tongue, mane, paws, skin, trunk, wings*

Review

Students roleplay a radio phone-in on an environmental issue. The arguments for and against will need to be discussed first. This also gives an opportunity to practise comparative and superlative adjectives.

Warmer

Students in groups think of an animal in English for every letter of the alphabet. You could make this into a team activity, with teams scoring one point for a correct name, and an extra point if the other team did not think of that animal. Include birds and fish. You will need to do some preparation on this yourself, or at least to have a good dictionary available.

1

Check students understand the meaning of *cartoons*. If they think of Walt Disney they should be able to think of a lot of examples. Write the examples under the four headings on the board afterwards, and get students to explain. Examples: Bugs Bunny is a cartoon rabbit. We can make shoes and handbags from crocodile skin. We use rats, birds, mice, etc in scientific experiments. People race each other on horseback. Let group representatives report back to the class.

2

Elicit the names of the animals first: *crocodile, lizard, python*. Give students a few minutes to work in groups or pairs and write some ideas of what they think the story is about. As usual with such activities, they should make their initial guesses before they read the text. If students ask: *tracking* = following; *arsenal* = place where guns, etc are kept, also used of a collection of weapons; *trapped* = not able to get out; *authorities* = government; *to locate* = to find. However, they are reading for gist, not detail, at this stage.

3

Students work in pairs and, after the exercise, guess why the man had the animals and the weapons and what he was doing in the USA. Extend the activity by roleplaying a police interview with the tenant. The police officer takes notes and then both students write up the police report using a mixture of direct and reported speech. Students could look at Language Summary 1 on practice page 91 and do the exercise on reported speech first.

Answers
2 *a glass cupboard* 3 *the bath* 4 *Germany*
5 *a historian* 6 *the United States* 7 *a police investigator*

4

Tell students to discuss the pictures in groups.

Answers
1 *The St Bernard dog – trained by Swiss monks in the Alps in the 1600s. Famous for rescuing people in the mountains.*
2 *The American bald eagle – symbol of the USA. The eagle traditionally symbolizes strength, power and courage.*
3 *The cow – considered a sacred animal by Hindus in India and allowed to wander free.*

Before students attempt the second part of this activity, it may be helpful for them to do Exercise 3 on practice page 91. Make sure they understand all the words.

Answers
1 *four legs, hair, a long tail, paws, sharp teeth*
2 *beak, feathers, a long tail, wings*
3 *four legs, hair, horns, a long tail*

To extend the activity, ask students to work in small groups to suggest a different animal for each of the unused adjectives. If you want to make this a competition, allocate points in the same way as for the animal game in the Warmer.
You might want to give some additional words, eg, animals have *paws* or *hooves* (singular = *hoof*), but birds have *claws*.

5

 Play the cassette once. Students should be able to name the animals.
Play the cassette again for them to write down the key words. Let students discuss their answers in pairs after each listening.

UNIT 9 LESSON 2

Answers

	animal	key words
1	snake	long, thin, no legs, long tongue, dangerous, poisonous, smooth skin, lives in the grass
2	monkey	hairy, long tail, long arms, long arms, look like humans, live in trees, agile, eat nuts and fruit
3	penguin	can't fly, black and white, funny, walks from side to side, swims, lives in Antarctica
4	zebra	looks like a donkey, lives in Africa, black and white
5	elephant	very big and grey, big floppy ears, lives in Africa and India, long trunk

If students have not already done Exercise 3 on practice page 91, now is a good time to do it.

6

Either complete this activity as directed in the lesson or give ten minutes for pairs to write their animal descriptions. Collect all the descriptions, number and display them round the classroom. Students have to identify all the animals.
Extend the activity by getting students to correct another pair's writing. If they keep their notes, they could use them for their homework.

7

Put students into groups of four for the interviews. Encourage them to take notes. Rearrange the students into new groups for them to compare answers. Find out which animal people find the most interesting by a show of hands.
Again, if students make notes on this activity they can use them for their homework.

Homework

If possible students should be encouraged to do some research in an encyclopaedia or reference book. Perhaps make a classroom wall display with drawings or magazine pictures of the various animals. Prepare the homework by doing a class description together in class. Students can also use any notes they made in Activities 6 and 7. They should write 100-150 words.

Practice *page 91*

Language Summary 1

If the topic is not new, elicit what students know about reported speech. Ask questions like:
What reporting verbs do we use?
What word usually follows the reporting verb?
What usually happens to the other verb?
What other words change?
Ask students to give examples. See how much the students can report from memory about the newspaper article in Lesson 2 Activity 2.

1

Then ask students to do the exercise alone or in pairs. Point out how ambiguity of pronouns should be avoided, hence the alternatives in brackets.

Answers
2 Reinstaedt said (that) the tenant was writing a military history book.
3 He said (that) they (the police) were still looking for him.
4 He said (that) the US authorities were helping with enquiries.
5 He said (that) he (the tenant) had over 50 weapons in his flat.
6 He said (that) he (the tenant) obviously liked animals too.
7 He said (that) there was a crocodile swimming in his (the tenant's) bath tub.
8 He said (that) he (the tenant) also had a large python in the hall.

Language Summary 2

If your students have been having problems with *say* and *tell*, go through Language Summary 2 with them. Then ask them to go through the text in Lesson 2 Activity 2, picking out the sentences with the two verbs in. Or you might like them to find the examples first, and try to draw their own conclusions before they look at the explanation.

2

Students do the exercise on their own or in pairs. Check the answers round the class.

Answers
1 *tell* 2 *say* 3 *say* 4 *say* 5 *tell* 6 *was saying/said* 7 *told*
8 *tell*

3

Students may want to work in pairs or small groups, discussing the words. Check pronunciation, and that they know the singular of *hooves* is *hoof*.
Extend this activity by asking students to find pictures of the animals they wrote descriptions of for homework, and label the parts of the body.

Answers
bird: wing, beak, feather
bull: tail, horn, hoof
lion: fur, ear, paw, fur

Lesson 3 *Nature at work*

Aims: To give students practice in talking about and listening to experiences in bad weather and in writing postcards.

Language focus

1 Short forms
Don't worry, we're OK.
Having a great time.

2 Past continuous for background description
We were staying in a horrible hotel next to the noisiest disco in the town.

Skills focus

- **Reading:** postcards for specific language and for detail
- **Writing:** postcards
- **Listening:** to a narrative for main idea and for detail

Vocabulary focus

- Climatic conditions: *flood(ed), typhoon, sandstorm, blizzard, fog, hurricane*
- Nature: *palm trees, waves, earthquake*

Review

Students in groups play twenty questions (see Unit 2, Lesson 2) about animals. One person thinks of an animal. The other students in the group ask *yes/no* questions (maximum 20) to discover its identity. Examples: *Does it have four legs? Can it fly?*

Warmer

Open the lesson with a brief class discussion about the weather. Ask them what their favourite weather is.

1

Brainstorm words students associate with each of the photos in Activity 1. Write them on the board and help with pronunciation. Students work in pairs to discuss the questions and report any interesting experiences back to the class.

2

If possible, turn out the classroom lights to heighten the effect of the sound sequence. Let students discuss the sounds in pairs or small groups. Provide any necessary vocabulary. Give the answer immediately – the fourth photo from the top, on the right – or wait until the students have heard Anthony's story in Activity 3 so that they can revise their predictions.

3

Give time for students to read the questions before they listen. If they ask, *hut* = small basic wooden house. They will also need to know *lift up* = raise; *went out* = stopped working; *huge* = very big; *terrified* = very frightened. You could revise the difference between *terrifying/terrified, frightening/frightened*, etc.
▣ Play the cassette once. Then allow students to discuss their answers in pairs. Now play the cassette again for students to answer the comprehension questions.
Finally, ask students how they would have felt and what they would have done in the situation.

Answers

1 *On an island in the south of the Philippines.*
2 *His girlfriend.*
3 *About two or three o'clock in the morning.*
4 *Because of the sound of the wind in the trees and the very heavy rain on the roof.*
5 *It was lifted up.*
6 *They went out.*
7 *He felt terrified, but he also enjoyed it.*
8 *It was covered in rubbish – wood, leaves, etc.*

You could go through Language Summary 2 on practice page 92 at this point, and the students could do Exercise 3.

4

Before students complete this activity, you may want to go through Language Summary 1 on practice page 92, and ask them to do Exercise 1. Encourage the students to underline the phrases/words that they think are different at the same time as they try to identify the true postcard.
▣ If they find the activity difficult, replay the cassette.

Answers

Anthony's postcard: A.
Differences in B: we've done lots of things; we stayed in bed.
Differences in C: didn't get any sleep; a window broke; lasted all day.

5

See if students can think of other types of writing where words are missed out, eg: telexes, notes, messages, newspaper headlines. If you have not already looked at Language Summary 1 on practice page 92, do so now. Students can do Exercise 1 on the same page. Students try to identify the missing words on their own, and then compare answers in pairs.

Answers

A *The holiday's great. It's too hot ... the temperatures ... We had an incredible experience ... We woke up ... We could see palm trees ... It was quite frightening ... I can't wait ...*
B *We want to stay ... We woke up ... We were so terrified ... I'll tell you more ...*
C *We are having ... It's really hot ... We didn't get any sleep ... We could hear ... It lasted all day. We'll see you soon. I hope you're feeling better.*

This would be a good time for students to do Exercise 2 on practice page 92.

6

This could be an oral story-telling activity, perhaps with each group recording their story, or a written group story where each group nominates a secretary and students take it in turns to suggest the next line.
Help students with the vocabulary in the box beforehand.

Homework

As preparation students would benefit from doing practice page 92 Exercises 1 and 2, if they have not already done so. Perhaps brainstorm possible positive and negative words to use to describe experiences. Write them up under two headings on the board, eg:
positive: *great fun, enjoyable, amazing, incredible, exciting*
negative: *boring, a waste of time, really expensive, terrible*
Also brainstorm the kind of things you write about on postcards, such as food, sights, weather, the people, etc.
As an additional activity, ask students to find a holiday picture they like from a magazine or holiday brochure and write a postcard, imagining they are on holiday there. This could be made into a wall display.

Practice *page 92*

1

Students do this exercise alone or in pairs. Make sure they are aware that *'d* can stand for *had* or *would* and that *'s* can stand for *is* or *has*.

Answers
2 *I would*   3 *let us*   4 *does not, it will*   5 *She has, it will*
6 *do not, he would*

2

Ask the students to read the postcard quickly for meaning. Ask a few gist questions to check comprehension:
Who wrote the card? Who did she write to? Where did she go?
Students do the task individually and compare answers in pairs. Elicit the contracted forms from the students before they rewrite the postcard since many of the contracted forms will be omitted in the final written version.

Answers
Hi Constance,
(We <u>are</u>) having a wonderful time here in Italy. (We) <u>have</u> been to Rome and (we) (<u>have</u>) visited the Roman ruins. (We <u>are</u>) hoping to go to Florence tomorrow. (I) <u>have</u> got a slight cold at the moment, but <u>do not</u> worry – it <u>will</u> soon go, I <u>am</u> sure. Ron <u>has</u> taken lots of photos with his new camera. (It <u>is</u> a) pity you <u>could not</u> come with us. Anyway, (we <u>are</u>) looking forward to seeing you.
Love Nicki.

Hi, Constance,
Having a wonderful time here in Italy. Have been to Rome and visited the Roman ruins. Hoping to go to Florence tomorrow. Have got a slight cold at the moment, but don't worry – it'll soon go, I'm sure. Ron's taken lots of photos with his new camera. Pity you couldn't come with us. Anyway, looking forward to seeing you.
Love Nicki.

3

As a lead-in you could replay the sound sequence from Lesson 3 Activity 2, and elicit a description from the class, encouraging students to correct each other. Write the sentences up on the board, eg:
It was raining hard. A strong wind was blowing. The hut was creaking.
Then students do Exercise 3.

Answers
2 *It was dark.*
3 *He couldn't believe he was alive.*
4 *It was raining very hard.*
5 *A strong wind was blowing.*
6 *He could see waves crashing against the rocks.*
7 *His clothes were very wet and torn.*
8 *He could hear strange noises, but couldn't see anything.*

4

Students do the first part of the exercise alone and check it in pairs.

Answers
freezing   cold   cool   warm   hot   boiling
Make sure they understand that *freezing* and *boiling* are often used to mean very cold, or very hot, and not just in their literal sense.
Tell students it may be easier for them to decide which column to put words in if they try to put them into a phrase, perhaps describing the climatic conditions in the photos in Lesson 3 Activity 1.

Answers

Adjectives	Nouns	Verbs
cloudy, cold, dry, foggy, hot, humid, sunny, wet, windy	drizzle, hail, rain, showers, snow, sunshine, wet, wind	drizzle, hail, rain, snow

Note: Although *cold* and *wet* are normally used as adjectives, there are expressions such as: *the intense cold, Don't go out in the wet.*

Unit 10 Into the unknown

The theme for this unit is exploration and adventure, leading up to students organizing their own expedition and asking for sponsorship in a formal letter.

Lesson 1 *The Blue Nile*

Aim: To give students practice in reading different texts and comparing them.

Language focus

1 *too* and *enough*
The water was too fast and dangerous for the dinghies.
Dave and Steve didn't think it was safe enough to continue.

2 Past perfect
Once the team had passed the falls, they put the dinghies back on the river.

Skills focus

• **Reading:** a factual narrative for main ideas and for detail
• **Speaking:** comparing information
• **Writing:** a diary page

Vocabulary focus

• Adventure: *single-handed, solo, explore, adventure, dinghy, to capsize, to drown, a bandit, a canoe, a rifle*
• Geographical features: *a whirlpool, a gorge, a waterfall, a cave*

Review

You may want to display the postcards the students wrote for their homework in Unit 9 Lesson 3.
Working in pairs or small groups, students prepare a brief statement about the weather now, and a short forecast for the next day or two.

1

This is a warmer activity for the topic of the lesson. Tell students not to worry if they do not know the correct vocabulary. They should discuss the photo in pairs or small groups. The groups report back to the class. You can either give them the words *dinghy* and *paddle* now, or wait until Activity 4.

Answer
The photo shows people in a dinghy, paddling down a river.

2

Again encourage discussion, before the students look at the passage. The Nile is now generally agreed to be the longest river in the world. (The Amazon is the second longest.)

Answers
b) The Nile is approximately 6,700 kilometres long, though experts disagree on its exact length. The Blue Nile, which is the focus here, rises in Ethiopia and runs through the Sudan where it joins the White Nile, which then passes through Egypt. Along the banks of the Blue Nile you can see snakes, crocodiles and turtles.

3

Tell students that they are going to read about two expeditions down part of the Blue Nile. Get them to speculate, again before they read the passage, what problems they might have in terms of food, water, weather, wildlife, navigation, etc. Then do the vocabulary exercise. Help students with the pronunciation of *canoe* – /kəˈnuː/ and *dinghy* – /ˈdɪŋɡɪ/ in particular.

Answers
2 – f   3 – a   4 – g   5 – d   6 – b   7 – h   8 – c

4

Give a time limit of about 15 minutes for students to read the text and complete the map. Make sure that they don't look at the other text if they finish early.

Answers

If students have problems with the past perfect tense, you may want to go through Language Summary 2 on practice page 93, and for students to do Exercise 2.

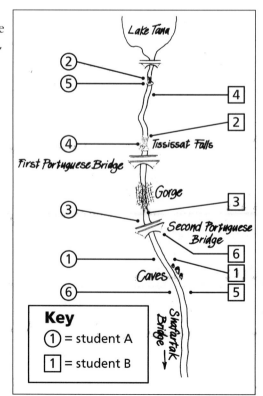

56

UNIT 10 LESSON 1

5
Allow a few minutes for students to complete the table. Again make sure they don't look at their partner's text and table. Since this is a jigsaw exercise, don't go over the answers until after the discussion in Activity 6.

Answers

	A	B
Expedition year	1968	1972
Expedition leader	John Blashford Snell	Mike Jones
Number of people	56	5
Starting date	8 September	3 September
Finishing date	25 September	12 September
Number of deaths	One	None

6
Tell students not to let their partner see their table or their text. Information must be exchanged orally by asking and answering questions. They can ask as many questions as they like about the story.
Encourage students to use the questions as a prompt for further comparison and discussion. Give an example of the sort of question the students should ask, eg (for the first question):
When did your expedition take place?

Homework
The students' speculations in Activity 4 would be good preparation for this. Students should date each entry, but they may have two or three short entries or one long one. If you like, remind them that diary language is often rather similar to postcard language, with omissions and abbreviations.
As an additional activity, roleplay a press interview with one or more members of either expedition. Make sure the interviewers have prepared at least four questions. Point out that *Wh-* questions usually get more interesting answers than *yes/no* questions.

Practice *page 93*

Language Summary 1
Ask students to find other examples of *too* and *enough* in the two reading texts in Lesson 1 Activity 4. Then explain the rule.

1
Students do the exercise alone or in pairs.
Extend the activity by asking them to write five sentences about themselves using too and enough, eg:
I'm too frightened to go rock-climbing.

Answers
2 *too – d* 3 *enough – e* 4 *enough – c* 5 *too – f* 6 *enough – a*

Language Summary 2
Write up the following two sentences on the board:
Once the team had passed the falls, they put the dinghies back on the river.
The team put the dinghies back on the river once they had passed the falls.
Ask students to identify the different verb forms and how they are made up. Ask them which action happened first in time in each sentence. Draw up the time line from the practice page if necessary to explain the difference between the past simple and the past perfect.

2
Then students do the exercise, working alone and checking in pairs or round the class.

Answers
2 *When she reached the check-in, she realized she had forgotten her passport.*
3 *She discovered the prices had gone up when she bought another ticket.*
4 *She discovered someone had taken her seat when she got on the plane.*
5 *When she arrived at Addis Ababa, she discovered the airline had lost her luggage.*
6 *When she arrived at the expedition headquarters, the expedition had left.*

3
Tell students to read the whole text before they fill in the gaps.

Answers
1 *At first* 2 *then* 3 *but* 4 *The next day* 5 *in the end* 6 *while*

4
Point out to students that although we may write *12(th) September 1961* we say, *the twelfth of September nineteen sixty-one*. Extend the activity by having a different starting date for the expedition and have a team quiz. See who can work out the dates the fastest.

Answers
2 *Friday 13th September*
3 *Saturday 7th September*
4 *Monday 9th September*
5 *Sunday 25th August*
6 *Monday 2nd September*
7 *Sunday 1st September*
8 *Sunday 8th September*

UNIT 10 LESSON 2

Lesson 2 Cycling across the Andes

Aims: To give students practice in listening to a personal account of an expedition; to plan an expedition of their own.

Language focus

1 *have to* and *must* for obligation
You have to calculate exactly how much water you need in the desert.
You must write a book about your trip.

2 Revision of the *-ing* form
We cycled past glaciers and saw them crashing into lakes.

3 Prepositions of movement and direction
We cycled through mountainous countryside and across salt flats.

Skills focus

- **Listening:** to a personal account in the past for main ideas and detail
- **Reading:** part of a magazine article for specific information
- **Speaking:** planning an expedition

Vocabulary focus

- Landscapes: *desert, jungle, salt flats, farmlands, forest*

Review

Display the diary pages for everyone to read. Then let pairs from different expeditions (in Lesson 1 Activity 5), who have not worked together, ask each other a few questions, eg:
How long were you in the water?
Or play a guessing game in teams, where one team thinks of an object, and the other asks questions about it. They must first ask questions using a comparative or superlative form, eg:
Is it as big as/bigger than a table?
They can then, if they wish, ask a second, information question, eg: *Is it an animal? Is it blue?*

Warmer

Students in groups see how many South American countries and capital cities they can name in three minutes.
Or write up the following qualities on the board:
fitness, patience, stamina, determination, intelligence, tolerance, bravery, fluency in other languages, initiative.
Students in groups decide on the three most important qualities for going on an expedition and give reasons, eg:
We think initiative is really important because when something goes wrong you can find a solution.

1

Tell students that this vocabulary will be necessary for the listening activity. They may use dictionaries if they need to, but they should try to guess the words if they can.

Answers
2 – *f*   3 – *e*   4 – *a*   5 – *d*   6 – *g*   7 – *b*

2

Give pairs a short time to discuss the questions and make a note of any landscape features they suggest.
After they have compared their answers, let some pairs report back to the class.

Answers
The Andes are the mountain chain that runs down the west side of South America, from Colombia, down through Ecuador, Peru, Bolivia, Chile and Argentina. The highest mountain is Acuncagua, which stands at nearly 7,000 metres. The Andes are also famous for the Inca ruins of Macchu Picchu in Peru, and the Valley of the Volcanoes in Ecuador, as well as for the condors, llamas, vicunas and alpacas that inhabit them.

Tell students they will have to listen to Eric's account for the different types of landscape.

3

Play the whole cassette once and let students discuss the text in pairs. Remind them to listen for landscape features only.

Answers
Eric mentions: a – mountains, d – salt flats, c – beaches, g – vineyards, f – glaciers.

4

Now play the cassette again, twice if necessary. This time students are listening for specific information.
Students compare answers in pairs. Encourage them to answer in complete sentences when they tell the class their answers, eg: *They started the expedition in August 1990.*

Answers

Starting date: August 1990	**Finishing date:** end of February 1991
Highest altitude: over 4,000m	**Lowest altitude:** sea-level
Length of time in Bolivia: 2 months Chile: 4 months Argentina: 1 month	
Total distance travelled: 4,200 miles or 6,700 kilometres	

UNIT 10 LESSON 2

5
Allow five minutes for students to make suggestions in groups with a group secretary writing ideas down. They may find some useful vocabulary in Lesson 1. Then the groups report back to the class. List the ideas on the board under headings such as cycling, weather, camping, people, etc.

6
Students read the text just looking for the ideas their group wrote down in Activity 5. Vocabulary students might find difficult: *a puncture* = a hole in the tyre; *a pump* = a tool to put air into the tyres; *frozen (water)* = ice.

7
This time the students have to read for specific, detailed information.

Answers
2 F – they were mostly technical   3 T   4 F   5 F   6 T   7 T

8
This should not be difficult for students to guess.
Ask them to give the answers in full sentences, eg:
Lina's best moment was when ...
Then play the cassette once. Let students discuss the answers in pairs.

Answers
Lina: Best moment – 1   Worst moment – 4
Biggest fear – 2   Future plans – 3
Eric: Best moment: camping near a glacier and seeing it crash into a lake.
Worst moment: Lina's bike broke down in high winds 80 miles from the nearest civilization.
Biggest fear: not being accepted by people – being robbed.
Future plans: cycle across central Asia from Mongolia to Pakistan.

9
Put students into groups of four or five. Give them ten minutes to agree on what they would like to do, where, and what six pieces of equipment they would take. Provide students with vocabulary such as *camping stove, tent, mosquito net, torch*, etc.
Then pair each student with a student from another group to let them exchange plans and give reasons for their choices of equipment.

Homework
Students should write about 100 words. Remind them that they can use the texts in Lesson 1 Activity 5 as a pattern. If necessary, play the relevant cassette extracts again, and encourage students to make notes. They might also get some ideas from Ted's second journey, in Unit 8, Lesson 2, Activity 3.

Practice *page 94*

Language Summary 1
Tell students to underline phrases in the reading text in Lesson 2 Activity 6 that refer to obligation or lack of obligation. Ask whether they refer to the past or the present. Write up the following expressions and explain that:
You mustn't camp here means it's a bad idea/not allowed, so don't.
You don't have to camp here means there is no obligation, but you can if you want.

1
Students can do the exercise alone and check the answers in pairs, as a dialogue.

Answers
2 had to   3 don't have to   4 had to
5 didn't have to/doesn't have to   6 must
7 must   8 must   9 mustn't
10 had to   11 must   12 mustn't

2
Tell students to do the exercise alone or in pairs.
Extend the activity by writing up the following words on the board: *birds, children, two men, cows, the snow, a police officer*. Students in pairs or groups make up example sentences using each word in turn and *-ing*, eg:
We saw birds flying high in the sky.
We could hear birds singing in the trees.

Answers
2 jumping   3 burning   4 blowing   5 darkening
6 falling   7 shouting 8 barking

3
Let students discuss the words in pairs. Then ask for the answers and write them up on the board.
Extend the activity by getting students to suggest other nouns for each adjective, eg: *dry desert, dry wine, dry weather, dry clothes; heavy rain, heavy luggage, heavy smoker/drinker*.

Answers
deep: sea, rivers, snow, water (*deep forest* is also possible, with the meaning of *thick*)
dry: desert
heavy: rain, snow
high: mountains; also *high rivers, sea*, suggest flooding; *high wind* = strong wind
icy: mountains, rain, rivers, sea, water, wind (Antarctica has also been described as an *icy desert*)
strong: wind
tall: forest, trees
thick: forest, snow, trees

UNIT 10 LESSON 3

Lesson 3 *Organizing an expedition*

Aims: To give students practice in planning an expedition and writing a formal letter requesting sponsorship.

Language focus

1 Revision of future forms
Present continuous: Our unit is sending a four-month expedition to Antarctica next spring.
going to: We are a team of six scientists who are going to visit Libya some time next year.
will: Unfortunately the expedition will be expensive.

2 *hope to* and *hope (that)*
We hope to go to India next year.
We hope (that) you will be able to support us.

Skills focus

- **Speaking:** Discussing and organizing an expedition
- **Reading:** formal letters for main ideas and to analyse style
- **Writing** a formal letter

Vocabulary focus

- Miscellaneous: *sponsorship, rare, a cure, a disease, an archaeologist, remains, excavation, support, valuable*

Review

Display the magazine articles the students wrote for their Lesson 2 homework around the room. Students should look at each other's work and suggest any corrections. Go through any general problems, drilling or giving extra practice as necessary.

1

Give students a couple of minutes to discuss the questions in pairs. If they ask, *sponsorship* = financial support, given by an organization or an individual; *a foundation trust* = a fund of money to which people may apply for financial support for a particular purpose.

Answer
The Adventure Foundation Trust put the advertisement in the paper to encourage people needing money for an expedition to apply for sponsorship.

2

Make sure students understand the vocabulary in the four letters: *rare* = not common; *a cure* = a remedy, making someone/something better; *a disease* = a serious illness. This activity is for gist reading practice so only allow two to three minutes.

Answers
1 C   2 D   3 A   4 B

3

Put students into groups of three or four. Allow ten to fifteen minutes for discussion in groups. Suggest to students that they make notes on each expedition in answer to each of the questions before they discuss fully which expedition to sponsor.
Help with vocabulary: *to support* = to help; *to cover* = to pay for; *valuable* = important.
Go round monitoring the discussions and making sure students have reasons for their choices.
Let each group report back to the class. Note how many groups support each expedition. Are their reasons the same?

4

Perhaps change the groups for the second part of the lesson. Allow 15-20 minutes for students to plan. Ask each group to appoint a secretary to take notes. Tell them that they will need the notes later. Remind them that they may find useful ideas in Lessons 1 and 2, and also in Unit 8 (Ted's two expeditions).

5

If students are not familiar with formal letters you might like to do Exercise 4 on practice page 95 first.
Allow ten minutes for discussion.

Answers
Good address layout: B or C
date: D
greeting: A
first sentence: A
last sentence: C or B
ending: A

UNIT 10 LESSON 3

6
Before students start to write their letter, you may wish to go through Language Summary 1 on practice page 95, to revise the future, and Language Summary 2, uses of *hope*. As this may not be familiar to students, they should do Exercise 2. Tell students to use their notes from Activity 4, and use the letters in Activity 2 (good points only, of course) and on practice page 95 as models.

Follow-up: Have a class competition to decide which expedition deserves the money most. Either display the letters round the classroom and students circulate and vote (but not for their own). Or each group makes a presentation of their expedition, and then the class votes. This would be useful preparation for the homework.

Homework
Remind students to do a formal letter layout. The reply may be positive or negative, but should include reasons. The Trust need not offer all the money asked for.

Practice *page 95*

Language Summary 1
Tell students to identify all the verb forms referring to future time in the four letters in Lesson 3 Activity 2.
Then elicit the differences between *going to*, the present continuous and *will*. Point out that in most cases in this unit *going to* and the present continuous are interchangeable, but that we tend to use the present continuous when talking about a definite time, place, etc, whereas with *going to* the details may be less certain. We don't often use *going to* with the verb *to go*.

1
Answers
2 *are going*
3 *are flying*
4 *will probably do*
5 *will be*
6 *will be*
7 *won't rain*
8 *will be*
9 *are taking/are going to take*
10 *is going*
11 *are going*
12 *will have*

Language Summary 2
Refer students back to the letters in Lesson 3 Activity 2, to find examples of *hope*. Go through the explanation if necessary.

2
Students do the exercise alone or in pairs.
Extend the activity by getting them to write down three personal wishes – things they hope to do in the future, and three general wishes – things they hope will happen. Students discuss their hopes in groups.

Answers
2 *We hope to go for/stay three months.*
3 *I hope (that) it won't rain too much.*
4 *We hope to see/find the Snow Leopard.*
5 *We hope to do some plant studies.*
6 *I hope (that) the expedition won't be too expensive.*
7 *We hope to get sponsorship.*
8 *I hope (that) we get/take some good photographs.*
9 *I hope (that) we won't have any problems.*

3
Use this letter as a model for the homework in Lesson 3.

Answers
b – 6   c – 1   d – 5   e – 2   f – 3   g – 8   h – 4

ACCELERATE ELEMENTARY   TEST

Section 1: Comprehension
[20 marks]

**1 a Read the passage. Tick (✓) the title that is best.
    [2 marks]**

   1 Man on Mars
   2 Near ... but not near enough
   3 The space race

> Can you imagine it? You travel 384,403 kilometres on the trip of a lifetime – and when you finally arrive, you don't even get out and have a look round!
>
> You might laugh, but it can happen. Take poor old Michael Collins, for example. He was one of the three American astronauts on the Apollo 11 moon mission.
>
> On 20 July 1969, Apollo's landing capsule, the Eagle, touched down on the surface of the moon. For the first time in history humans had landed on another world!
>
> The world listened in amazement as the first words from the moon were heard on planet Earth. 'Tranquility base here,' astronaut Neil Armstrong told Mission Control. 'The Eagle has landed.'
>
> Then Armstrong stepped out of the capsule – the first man to walk on the moon. Shortly afterwards, crew-mate Edwin 'Buzz' Aldrin followed. The two of them spent almost three hours doing experiments, planting an American flag and taking photos.
>
> The footprints that Armstrong and Aldrin left on the moon are still there today. There is no wind on the moon to blow them away because the moon has no atmosphere. The astronauts also left behind several pieces of equipment, including cameras and spacesuit back-packs.
>
> Poor old Michael Collins wasn't in the Eagle, he had to stay in Apollo 11 for the whole trip. He didn't step out until the spacecraft came down safely in the Atlantic Ocean eight days after it left the Kennedy Space Centre in Florida.
>
> The Apollo landing was a major achievement and five other moon missions followed – the last was in 1972. Many people think that these were a waste of money and that America just wanted to win the 'Space race' against the former Soviet Union. On the other hand, we now know a great deal about the moon. Rock samples, for example, have helped to explain how and when the moon was formed.
>
> So was the moon landing worthwhile? I wonder what Michael Collins thinks about it!

**b Are these sentences true or false?
    Write T or F in the box. [10 marks]**

Example: Michael Collins didn't land on the moon. [T]
1 Three men were on the Apollo 11 mission. ☐
2 Armstrong and Aldrin were on the moon for under two hours. ☐
3 The two men took a flag to the moon with them. ☐
4 There hasn't been a mission to the moon since 1972. ☐
5 Apollo 11's mission lasted for five days. ☐

**c Write answers to these questions about the passage. You do not need to write complete sentences.
    [8 marks]**

1 What happened on 20 July, 1969?
_____
2 What kind of equipment was left on the moon?
_____
3 Why are the astronauts' footprints still on the moon?
_____
4 Where did Apollo 11 land when it returned to Earth?
_____

Section 2: Communication
[20 marks]

2 Write questions for these answers.

Example: _What do you do?_
I'm a student. I'm studying music.

1 _____
It's on July the 22nd.

2 _____
Yes, I do. It's my favourite drink.

3 _____
At the weekend? I'm visiting some friends in London.

4 _____
The nearest post office? There's one in Hope Street.

5 _____
One bottle, please.

6 _____
I was born in New Orleans.

7 _____
I started collecting stamps when I was a child.

8 _____
They've been living there for six months.

9 _____
Yes, of course. My home telephone number is 131718.

10 _____
I think it'll be cloudy and wet.

Section 3: Language [20 marks]

3 a Choose ten of these words to complete the first ten spaces in the conversation. Underline each word you choose. [10 marks]

Example: A aren't B don't C haven't
1 A best   B better   C good
2 A already B never C yet
3 A see B to see C seen
4 A saw B see C seen
5 A which B where C why
6 A could B must C should
7 A can't B mustn't C won't
8 A eating B going C having
9 A at B on C in
10 A long B many C much

b Complete the last ten spaces with your own words. Write one word in each space. [10 marks]

RICHARD: Why ___don't___ we go to the cinema one evening next week?
HELEN: That's a (1) _____ idea. What's on at the Apollo?
RICHARD: Interview with the Vampire, I think. I've (2) _____ seen it so I'd prefer (3) _____ something different. How about The Piano?
HELEN: OK, fine. I haven't (4) _____ it yet. Do you know (5) _____ it's on?
RICHARD: Just a minute. I'll look in the newspaper. It's on at the Phoenix until Thursday. We (6) _____ go on Tuesday.
HELEN: Sorry, I (7) _____ . I'm (8) _____ a meal with some friends on Tuesday. What about Wednesday?
RICHARD: Wednesday's no good for me, I'm afraid. I've got my Japanese lesson (9) _____ seven o'clock.
HELEN: How (10) _____ have you been learning Japanese?
RICHARD: Well, I've been teaching myself (11) _____ August. I've only (12) _____ three lessons with a teacher.
HELEN: Have you (13) _____ to Japan?
RICHARD: Yes, I was in Kyoto for two (14) _____ last year. It's (15) _____ second largest city in Japan.
HELEN: What were you (16) _____ there?
RICHARD: I was teaching English. I'd like to go back. I've just noticed – The Seven Samurai is also on at the Phoenix. It's (17) _____ old, black and white Japanese film. It (18) _____ made in 1954, I think.
HELEN: Fine. What time (19) _____ it start?
RICHARD: Nine o'clock. Why don't we go after my lesson?
HELEN: OK, let's do that, then. I'll meet (20) _____ outside the cinema.

Section 4: Writing [20 marks]

4 Write a letter to a friend. Describe some things you have done since you last wrote to your friend. Talk about some of your plans for the future. Write at least six sentences.

Dear, _____

ACCELERATE ELEMENTARY TEST — TO THE TEACHER

To the Teacher

Each of the four levels of *Accelerate* is accompanied by a test, which consists of:

- a *To the teacher* section
- photocopiable worksheets for students
- an answer key

The tests can serve two purposes.

1 Diagnostic. The tests can be used to enable the teacher to assess the level of a class as a whole and to identify general areas of weakness before students begin the course.

2 Achievement. The tests can be used to allow both students and teacher to identify progress made during the course. Students can repeat the test upon completion of their course even if they have already taken the same test at the beginning; in this way they can assess their improvement.

Each test is divided into six parts. These are:

1 Comprehension
2 Commnication
3 Language
4 Writing
5 Dictation (optional)
6 Oral task (optional)

Each section of the test carries 20 marks. The marks can be adjusted by the teacher, with greater or less emphasis given to particular sections.

Optional Section 5: Dictation [20 marks]

Tell students that you are going to dictate five sentences. Explain that you will read each sentence three times. First, read each sentence at normal speed. Then read the sentences slowly, breaking them up into phrases. Finally, read the sentences once more at normal speed.

4 marks for each sentence. Deduct one mark for each mistake.

1 There was nobody else in the house.
2 I've got a leather bag with a shoulder strap.
3 You will be healthier if you take more exercise.
4 One disadvantage of living in a city is that it's noisy.
5 I was allowed to watch television after I'd done my homework.

Optional Section 6: Speaking Task [20 marks]

Students work in pairs. Give each student a copy of the task. If you wish, you could try to record each conversation so that you can assess students' work at a later point in time.

Tell students what you will take into consideration when assessing their oral work. Criteria should include:

- fluency: speaking without too much hesitation [4 marks]
- grammatical accuracy: speaking without too many mistakes [4 marks]
- pronunciation: making individual sounds correctly, using stress, rhythm and intonation appropriately [4 marks]
- vocabulary: using a wide range of appropriate vocabulary [4 marks]
- communication: being able to ask questions, give opinions/advice etc [4 marks]

Speaking Task

Choose a book or film you have enjoyed. Be prepared to tell your partner about the book/film and to say why you liked it.

Work with your partner. Find out about the book/film your partner has chosen. Say if you have read/seen it or if you would like to. Find out if you like the same kind of books/films.

ACCELERATE ELEMENTARY TEST — ANSWERS

Section 1: Comprehension
[20 marks]

1 a 2 marks for the correct answer.

  b 10 marks: 2 marks for each correct answer.

   1 T 2 F 3 T 4 T 5 F

  c 8 marks: 2 marks for each correct answer. Do not deduct marks for notes rather than complete sentences. Suggestions include:

   1 the first man/men (Neil Armstrong and Edwin 'Buzz' Aldrin) landed on the moon
   2 cameras, spacesuit back-packs
   3 there is no wind to blow them away (because the moon has no atmosphere)
   4 in the Atlantic Ocean

Section 2: Communication
[20 marks]

2 2 marks for each question. Deduct one mark for each mistake. Any correct question is acceptable. Suggestions include:

   1 When's your birthday/the wedding etc?
   2 Do you like beer/wine/water etc?
   3 What are you doing at the weekend?
   4 Where can I find the nearest post office?/Where's the nearest post office?
   5 How much water etc would you like?/How many bottles of water etc do you want?
   6 Where were you born?/Can you tell me where you were born?
   7 When did you start collecting stamps?
   8 How long have they been living there?
   9 Could you give/tell me your (home) telephone number?/Can I phone you at home?
   10 What will the weather be like (in ...)?/What do you think the weather will be like (in ...)?

Section 3: Language
[20 marks]

3 a 10 marks: 1 mark for each correct answer.

   1 C 2 A 3 B 4 C 5 B 6 A 7 A 8 C 9 A 10 A

  b 10 marks: 1 mark for each appropriate answer. Suggestions include:

   11 since 12 had 13 been 14 days/weeks/months
   15 the 16 doing/teaching 17 an 18 was 19 does/will
   20 you

Section 4: Writing
[20 marks]

You might like to tell students what you will take into consideration when marking their written work. Criteria should include:

- efficient communication of meaning [7 marks]
- grammatical accuracy [7 marks]
- coherence in the ordering of the information or ideas [3 marks]
- capitalisation and punctuation [3 marks]

It is probably better not to use a rigid marking system with the written part of the test. If, for example, you always deduct a mark for a grammatical mistake, you may find that are over-penalising students who write a lot or who take risks. Deduct marks if students haven't written the minimum number of sentences stated in the test.

Tapescripts

Unit 1, Lesson 1, Activity 1

Interviewer: Brigitte, you're going to tell us about one of your festivals ... what's the name of the festival?
Brigitte: It's called Kermes.
Interviewer: And where does this festival take place?
Brigitte: It usually takes place in Germany and Austria.
Interviewer: And what time of year?
Brigitte: Well, it's at the end of August, beginning of September.
Interviewer: Right, and does everyone take part in this celebration?
Brigitte: Er, yes, mostly the whole family, it's very attractive for young people especially, but usually the whole family goes there because it takes place in the countryside where the farmers have just brought in the harvest, you see, so it's mostly a celebration in the countryside in small villages.
Interviewer: Does it take place in the cities too?
Brigitte: No, it doesn't. But people from the town go to the villages and take part.
Interviewer: So, this is when the harvest has been brought in by the farmers?
Brigitte: Yes that's right, and the crops and grapes and everything have just been brought in.
Interviewer: Right, what happens at the Kermes festival?
Brigitte: Well, usually there is a big beer tent, where people gather together, come together, and there are different musical groups. There's dancing, there's German, typical German, Austrian er, big sausages and potato salads, mustards, a whole lot of beer and wines, you know, and people enjoy it.
Interviewer: And they dance until the early hours?
Brigitte: They dance until the early morning, right, four, five, six in the morning, and this goes on for a few weeks. It takes place in different towns, sorry not towns, villages.
Interviewer: Yes.

Unit 1, Lesson 2, Activity 5

The festival called Odalan, that's O-D-A-L-A-N, takes place on the island of Bali in Indonesia. It happens once every Balinese year, usually every 210 days. It is celebrated by everyone, adults and children. It can last from one to seven days and is a festival to celebrate the birthday of the village temple, or church. The women of the village wear their most beautiful clothes and carry offerings of food, fruit and flowers to the temple. There is a short prayer service and music. In the evenings there is traditional dancing at the temple. On the last day of the festival, a model of the lion god Barong is carried in a procession through the village.

Unit 1, Lesson 3, Activity 1

1
Man: What do you think about picture 1? What's happening?
Woman: Well, I'm not sure. Umm ... all these people are looking at the woman so I think she's doing something wrong. Is she laughing?
Man: No, I don't think so. She's holding something in her hand. I think it's a tissue. I think she's sneezing.
Woman: Oh, you're right! She's sneezing in a place where there are lots of people – she's sneezing in public. That's a rude thing to do in Japan.
Man: OK. Good. So picture 1 is Japan.

2
Man: And picture 2. What's happening in this one?
Woman: Well, again, there are people looking at someone. This time they're eating a meal. A Chinese meal. What else is happening?
Man: Well, they're eating and there's a bowl of rice in the middle of the table. Em, the man is putting something into the rice bowl. What's he holding? Oh, what do you call those things that he's holding?
Woman: Oh, chopsticks. They're called chopsticks. So he's putting his chopsticks into the bowl of rice that everybody is using. That's the rude thing. So picture 2 is China.

3
Man: Picture 3.
Woman: Um, I don't know what's happening here. There are two people sitting down.
Man: Yes, and one is very relaxed. The other one looks, I don't know, angry maybe. In Thailand it's rude to point your feet at someone. I think that's what's happening here. Look at the feet. This man is pointing his feet at the other person and so he's looking angry.
Woman: That's right. Picture 3 is Thailand then.

4
Man: So picture 4 is India – that's the only country left.
Woman: Yes, and again people are eating. Eating an Indian meal. What's the woman doing?
Man: Well, she's eating, eating some bread I think. But these people aren't eating. They're looking at the woman.
Woman: But they're all holding some food.
Man: Yes. They're all doing the same thing.
Woman: Um ... no, they're not. Look. All these people are eating with the same hand. This woman isn't. She's eating with her left hand, not with her right.
Man: So that's the answer. It's rude to eat with your left hand in India.

Unit 2, Lesson 1, Activity 3

1
Woman: Here we are ... fiction ... oh it's so difficult to choose ...
Man: Ah ... the new Roddy Doyle novel – let's get Phil this. He's read all of his other books. They're really good stories – I read them all in two weeks!
Woman: That's a great idea! This is his latest novel and it's only just come out – Phil will love it! I'll just go and pay.

2
Woman: Have you decided what you'd like yet?
Man: Um ... nearly ... it's all so good, I've been here several times and the food's always excellent – it's hard to choose.
Woman: Yes, I know what you mean – I think I'll have the Neapolitan pizza and a beer ...
Man: Um ... are you having a starter?
Woman: No, the pizzas are really big here ... and the pasta is delicious too ...
Man: Right. I'll have the lasagne and a side salad – and I think I'll have a glass of red wine. Now, where's the waiter ...

3
Man 1: Excuse me, could you tell me when the last train leaves from here on the southbound Piccadilly line?
Man 2: Southbound Piccadilly? ... that's 12.20, sir ... from platform six.
Man 1: 12.20 platform six. Thanks a lot.

4
Man: Excuse me, do you have any maps of South America, not including Central America?
Woman: The South America section is near the stairs on the right.
Man: Yes, I've had a quick look, but I really want a map with the mountains in more detail – the ones over there just show the main roads.
Woman: Right, I'll come over and have a look. Perhaps you'd be better in the mountaineering section. The maps we have there are especially for climbers and I think there'll be something for South America.

Unit 2, Lesson 2, Activity 4

Sue: Right. We're going to play the twenty questions game. I choose an object in this room, somewhere in this room, and you can ask twenty questions to guess what it is. But I can only say yes or no. OK, ask me a question.
Tracy: Is it made of glass?
Sue: Um, no.
Luke Is it made of plastic?
Sue: Yes.
Tracy: Can anybody use it?
Sue: Yes, I think so.
Tracy: Can you use it, er ... do you have to use it only in a classroom?
Sue: No.
Luke: It is mechanical?
Sue: Yes.
Tracy: Ah, it's mechanical. Can you use it outside, er, in a garden?
Sue: Yes, yes you can.
Luke: Does it need electricity?
Sue: Sometimes, yes.
Tracy: It's mechanical, plastic, um.
Luke: Does it make a noise?
Sue: Yes.
Tracy: Ah, does it make a noise by itself?
Sue: Yes, you're getting very warm, very close.
Luke: Very close. Is it, um, a TV?
Sue: No, it's not a television.
Luke: Does it have buttons?
Sue: Yes.
Tracy: Can you turn it on and off?
Sue: Yes.
Tracy: Um, how many questions is that?
Sue: That's 13. You've got seven left.
Tracy: OK, let's see. And it's in this room.
Sue: Yes, definitely.
Tracy: It's in this room, something mechanical.
Luke: Um, the stereo system?
Sue: Yes, got it Luke. Right. Well done. OK, your turn.

TAPESCRIPTS

Unit 2, Lesson 3, Activity 4

1
African Experience Wildlife Park gives you a more interesting day out – for all the family.
See African wildlife from the comfort of your car and imagine you're on safari. If you look carefully, you will see monkeys, elephants, giraffes, lions and zebras and many others. We have a wider variety of animals than before.
African Experience Wildlife Park – a more enjoyable animal experience for all the family. Just off the M6 near Stoke-on-Trent.

2
Have you tried Hobson's yet? If you want bread and cakes that are fresher than at the supermarket and straight from the oven, you'll find them at Hobson's, now with a bigger selection to choose from!
Hobson's Bakery – open 9 to 5.30, six days a week for tastier bread and cakes.
Hobson's Bakery – see you there!

3
Need a holiday? Always wanted to go somewhere more exciting than Europe? Contact the Sunshine Company – THE travel agents for all your holiday requirements. We cover all popular locations in the Far East at cheaper prices than last year with an even better choice of hotels. And if you book a holiday with us this month, we will give you a 10% discount ... yes, that's 10% off your holiday price. So come and see The Sunshine Company – contact the specialists for a sunnier holiday in the Far East!

Unit 2, Lesson 3, Activity 5

Woodbridge Sport and Leisure Centre offers you a more interesting way to spend your leisure time with an even bigger selection of sports facilities than you can imagine. Try squash, badminton, indoor tennis and football or attend one of our exercise classes – we have a wider variety, all with fully-qualified instructors. We also have facilities for more exciting sports such as scuba diving and rock climbing. Now that summer's here and the weather is sunnier, why not swim in our outdoor pool? If you want a more enjoyable way to spend your free time, you will find something here at Woodbridge Sport and Leisure Centre. We have a better choice of sports all at cheaper prices than our competitors. Woodbridge Sports and Leisure Centre, just off the A10 south of Woodbridge. See you there!

Unit 3, Lesson 1, Activities 4 and 5

Interviewer: So, where do you live exactly?
Sheika: At Puerto Ayura on the island of Santa Cruz.
Interviewer: And that's one of the largest islands?
Sheika: Um. ... It's the second largest island on the Galapagos archipelago and it's the most populated island because of the tourism. All the tourism is in Santa Cruz.
Interviewer: And how long have you lived there?
Sheika: Oh, about two years.
Interviewer: And what do you do?
Sheika: I work as a naturalist guide.
Interviewer: Oh, lovely. Tell me, what do you like about living on the islands?
Sheika: Oh, first the simplicity of the life there. You don't have the same problems as in the big cities. Also, you have contact with nature all the time.
Interviewer: OK, perfect. Tell me what kind of problems do you have living in the islands? Someone told me that there's actually no fresh water available.
Sheika: Oh, yes. Yes, there isn't enough fresh water available and so if you make coffee it tastes salty because of the sea water.
Interviewer: Ooh, salty coffee. Ugh!
Sheika: Ah ... yes, but now we have a little bit of fresh water from the mainland.
Interviewer: Right. Any other problems?
Sheika: With the light ... with electricity. There's only one electricity generator, so you only have light until twelve o'clock at night. Oh, the other problems are that there's no TV and there's only one radio station.
Interviewer: Mmm ... how about cinemas, anything like that?
Sheika: Yes, that's a problem too. There's a cinema in Puerto Ayura, but only one, and it shows very old films.
Interviewer: Yeah. Any problems with transportation – like buses or cars?
Sheika: Well now there are relatively a lot of cars, about 8,000 cars in all the archipelago, in all the inhabited islands, but there's only one bus.
Interviewer: Right, just one bus ... gosh!
Sheika: Yes, so people always go around on bicycles.
Interviewer: Ah, right. Education and schools ... any problems with that?
Sheika: About education ... there's not really a problem with primary education ... I mean school. But there's no high school ... no secondary school for older children.
Interviewer: Right.
Sheika: Most people don't think about the problems of living on the Galapagos. People who live there don't care about the problems really, they just love the solitude and the freedom.
Interviewer: Yeah, that's the advantage of living there.
Sheika: Yes, yes ... sure.
Interviewer: Well, thank you for talking to us.

Unit 3, Lesson 2, Activity 4

They quickly decided that the rowing boat was going to pull the boat they were in, so they put up a sail.
At first Robin and Neil were seasick. Luckily, Lyn was a nurse, so she knew which pills to give them from the first-aid box.
On Day three Sandy caught their first fish. They cut it up and put it in the lemon juice which 'cooked' it. When they had no more lemons, they ate raw fish.
On Day seven, Douglas killed a turtle so they had ten kilos of meat, which they dried in the sun.
Sharks smelt the turtle blood and came to the boats. From then on sharks followed them all the time.
They had been on the life raft for two weeks. It had lots of holes in it and was always wet. So on Day 17 they moved into the rowing boat, which was drier.
After they moved into the rowing boat, there was a very bad storm.
They were very short of drinking water after the storm. On Day 38 Douglas saw a ship coming towards them and lit a flare.
A Japanese fishing boat saw the flare and rescued them. They were 600
miles off the coast of Panama.

Unit 3, Lesson 3, Activity 2

Part 1
1 The snakes are near south point.
2 The swamp is in the south west of the island between South Point and the reef.
3 The jungle is opposite Skull Island.
4 The volcano is in the centre of the island.
5 The beach is in the west of the island around Safe Bay.
6 The river runs from the inlet to Black Rock.
7 The skeleton is in the swamp.

Part 2
8 The piranhas are in the river.
9 The crocodiles are south of the reef.
10 The mountains are in the east of the island, between the reef and Skull Island, near the coast.

Unit 4, Lesson 1, Activity 4

Narrator: Rob has loved Cindy since he met her, but she isn't interested in him. The band has been the most important thing in Cindy's life for a long time. Tony signed the contract and the band are going to the studio on Thursday at 10 o'clock to record their song. On Tuesday they meet at Cindy's flat. Tony's sister Lucy is there too. The song is not perfect. Lucy tells Cindy that Rob has been unhappy for weeks because of her. Rob and Lucy go out to get some Chinese food, and Tony and Cindy listen to the tape. Lucy comes back without Rob and tells Tony something. They both look worried.

Unit 4, Lesson 2, Activity 2

Tony: I can't believe it. What are you saying?
Lucy: Oh, Rob didn't look ... He, he just stepped into the road and and the car hit him! Oh, it happened so quickly, Tony. One minute he was fine and the next minute he was lying on the ground.
Cindy What is it? What's the matter?
Lucy: It's Rob. He's had an accident. He's, he's dead, Cindy!
Narrator: Rob was dead! The shock was too great for Cindy and she fainted.
Tony: She looks awful. Ww ... will she be alright?
Lucy: Poor Cindy. Rob was in love with Cindy you see. He wrote his latest song for her. But Cindy wasn't interested in him. Well that's what she said ... and now it's too late.
Tony: [to himself] Oh, so that's why Rob was so worried. I love Cindy too. But I can never tell her now.
I, I ... I'll go and call a doctor! Where's the nearest phone box?
Lucy: Just a minute Tony – she's opening her eyes. Look stay here and help me.
Cindy: Oh ... What happened? Where am I?
Narrator: Then Cindy remembered ... Rob was dead.
Cindy: Oh no, Rob's dead! He's, he's dead ... and it's my fault. Rob, oh, Rob!
Tony: It's not your fault Cindy. Why is it your fault?
Lucy: Listen, Cindy, it was an accident. He just stepped into the road without looking. We came out of the take-away ... we started to cross the road ... and he just didn't look.
Cindy: I was so awful to him. It's my fault.
Tony: Come on, Cindy, you weren't awful to Rob. Don't say things like that. Don't cry.

67

TAPESCRIPTS

Narrator: But Cindy didn't stop crying. Her friends didn't know what to do. Lucy made her a cup of tea but Cindy didn't want to drink it. She wanted to be alone.
Tony: I'll have to phone Brock in the morning and tell him about Rob. We can't go to the recording studio on Thursday now.
Lucy: Come on, Tony, it's very late. Let's go home. Cindy wants to be alone now. Let's go.
Cindy: Why was I so horrible to Rob? Why was I so awful? He wrote that last song for me. I never want to sing it again. Oh Rob!
Narrator: Time passed but Cindy still felt bad about Rob's death. She didn't want to see Tony or Lucy. She wanted time to think.
Cindy: [to herself] Rob died two months ago ... but I still feel awful. It was all my fault. Why didn't I listen to him? He loved me and I didn't give him a chance. I don't want to sing with the band again. It's not the same without Rob. He tried to tell me what he felt through his songs. Why didn't I listen to him, I was really stupid. Oh Rob, I can't believe you're dead. It can't be true. I'm really sorry. I'd like to tell you that now, but it's too late.

Unit 4, Lesson 2, Activity 5

Narrator: The next day Cindy listened to Rob's last song ... the song he wrote for her.
Cindy: [to herself] Perhaps Lucy's right, I am selfish. I hurt Rob ... and now I'm doing the same thing to Tony. I'm hurting him too. Tony needs me. So I'll meet him and talk to him.
Narrator: Cindy met Tony the next day.
Tony: The record company still want us to make a record. I've got an appointment with Brock next week.
Cindy: Yes, I know Tony, Lucy told me.
Tony: We can start the band again ... just, just the two of us. We can change our name to DUO. We've already got some great songs, haven't we?
Cindy: Yes ... Rob's last song was really beautiful. I'm sorry Tony, but I can't sing Rob's songs now. His songs have a special meaning for me. I can't sing without Rob, can't you understand that?
Tony: Don't cry, Cindy, I understand. Rob's songs were special to you. I know that. I'll find another person for the band.
Cindy: I'd like to help Tony, but what can I do?
Narrator: On the way back to her flat, Cindy tried to explain.
Cindy: Rob's last song was a message for me. It was a beautiful song. A love song. I don't want to sing it again because he can't hear it.
Tony: I see.
Cindy: Well, goodnight Tony, it was nice to see you again. I'm sorry about the band. I hope you understand.
Tony: What about a a kiss for good luck Cindy?
Narrator: Cindy liked Tony. In some ways he was a brother to her, but this kiss was something more. Then Cindy remembered Rob. Why was she kissing Tony? What was she doing?
Cindy: No, Tony, stop it, I can't.
Tony: But Cindy, what's the matter?
Narrator: Quickly Cindy opened the door and rushed into her flat. She started to cry.
Cindy: [to herself] Oh no! I can't get involved with Tony. Not after Rob's death. Oh Rob, I hurt you so much. I'll never forget your last song ...
The words are beautiful Rob, it's your best song.

Rob: It's not difficult to write love songs. I just think of you. I close my eyes and think of you.
Cindy: You mustn't talk like that Rob, we've got to think of the band.
Rob: Is Trio the most important thing in your life, Cindy?
Cindy: Yes, Rob, it is. I've always put the band first.
Rob: Can't you think about anything else? Oh, Cindy, can't you understand what I'm trying to tell you.
Cindy: [to herself] Rob, Rob, I'm so sorry, come back and tell me again.

Unit 4, Lesson 3, Activity 1

Narrator: Two weeks later, Lucy came round to Cindy's flat again.
Lucy: Oh, you've got to go out more, Cindy. Staying at home all the time isn't good for you.
Cindy: Stop worrying about me Lucy, I'm alright. How's Tony?
Lucy: Not too bad, he's going on tour next month – to Manchester, Liverpool and Birmingham.
Cindy: What? With another singer?
Lucy: No, he didn't find another singer. He's going solo. He's giving his first concert at the Roxy on Friday.
Cindy: Oh, that's good. I'm really pleased for him. But he'll be nervous on his own.
Lucy: Yes, and he's got a real problem with one song. He just can't get it right. It's Rob's last song – you know the one he wrote before he ...
Cindy: ... before he died. Do you mean this one?
Narrator: Cindy picked up her guitar and started to sing.
Cindy: I can't live without your love.
Lucy: [to herself] It's a beautiful song ... why didn't Rob write it for me? Ah, but only Cindy can sing it. Cindy doesn't want to sing again. That's what she said. Perhaps she'll change her mind and help Tony now.
Narrator: Cindy didn't change her mind. But on Friday night she thought about Tony's first concert.
Cindy: [to herself] Is Tony's concert tonight or tomorrow night? Oh, It's tonight. It starts at 9 o'clock. Poor Tony – he'll be so nervous.

Unit 4, Lesson 3, Activity 2

Narrator: So Cindy decided to go along to the Roxy and watch Tony.
Cindy: [to herself] I'll go and watch him ... he'll never know ... I'll stand at the side, he won't see me.
Narrator: When she got to the Roxy, Brock was there.
Brock: Don't go in there Cindy, Tony's terrible tonight. What's the matter with him?
Cindy: What are you talking about?
Narrator: Lucy saw Cindy with Brock and came over to join them.
Brock: He wants to make a record! I don't believe it! I'm going home.
Cindy: [to herself] Why was I so selfish? Why didn't I help him?
Lucy: Oh, listen to him. Poor Tony. Oh, he needs your help Cindy.
Tony: To finish I'd like to sing a love song. A good friend of mine wrote it for a girl. We both loved her ... and I still do. It's called 'I can't live without your love'. This song is for Cindy ... and I want her here with me tonight.

Cindy: [to herself] What's Tony saying? I don't want to hear Rob's song. Oh, Tony.
Tony: I can't live without your love.
Narrator: Cindy remembered Rob's words.
Rob: I close my eyes and think of you.
Narrator: But Rob was dead ... And Tony needed her now.
Lucy: Hey! Come back! Where are you going?
Cindy: I know what's important. It's the singer not the song.
Tony: Cindy, I ...
Cindy: Don't stop singing Tony, this is a beautiful song. Let's sing it together.
Narrator: So Cindy sang with Tony. The words were beautiful. Cindy's voice was lovely and Tony was really happy. Everyone could see – and hear – the difference.
Brock: That sounds great! They're a fantastic duo. I'll go and book the recording studio now.
Lucy: No, book the studio tomorrow ... just listen to that song now. Cindy and Tony are great together. And now they'll be together forever.

Unit 5, Lesson 1, Activity 4

Well ... er ... I spent a lot of my childhood overseas, living overseas. Um ... we were ... er ... a family of three. I was an only child. Erm ... we always had lots of cats and dogs, and they were like brothers and sisters to me. Erm ... I come from a big family generally – I have lots of cousins. I've got twenty seven cousins. Erm ... I always wanted a big brother er when I was little. I could ... I'd still quite like a big brother. Erm ... I used to have lots of imaginary brothers and sisters and imaginary friends. Erm ... because I was an only child I, I got lots of presents. I was very spoilt um ... lots of fuss made over me. Erm ... I suppose on the other hand, erm ... sometimes I was lonely, I had erm ... a, a very good imagina ... imaginary life, erm ... I used my imagination a lot erm ... and now I suppose erm .. I would ... I would like to have brothers and sisters now ... erm ... partly because now my parents are older and I ... um ... know that as they get more older and maybe ill the responsibility will be mine.

Um ... I won't have anybody to share that responsibility. I think that's ... that's the main drawback.

Unit 5, Lesson 2, Activity 3

Jane: Well, we had a lot of rules, but a few of them were leaving the house without permission. That was forbidden. Er ... we weren't allowed to play with um ... children in the street who weren't (because my father was in the military) who weren't like us. And ... erm ... we had to always be home on time.
Interviewer: Do you think it was a good idea to have strict parents?
Jane: Well personally I don't, no, because I think that children and teenagers are rebellious and this kind of strictness it makes them more rebellious.
[PAUSE]
Brendan: There were quite a few really. Er ... for instance, you couldn't eat between meals. You ... you couldn't have little snacks and that, erm ... and if you did you'd ... you'd get hit and you might not then be served dinner that same evening – erm ... really to teach you er ... not to eat between meals, because if you did miss your dinner then of course you'd be

hungry all night, and this would teach you. So... Er... the other thing is that you, you had to eat whatever meals were put in front of you. If you didn't, they were served cold the next time, and until it was finally cleared you never got a new meal. It was the same stuff served up all the time, and cold as well. Which was something awful.

Interviewer: Do you think your parents were quite strict?

Brendan: Erm ... I, I think my mother was. My father probably was er ... more easy going, but, but my mother was quite strict.

Interviewer: And was this a good thing?

Brendan: Um ... oh I ... it depends. I think it was ... yes, I think it was.

Unit 5, Lesson 2, Activity 4

Jane: Well I was fifteen, and I was a very difficult teenager, and this was my first rock festival. So I went to the ro ... rock festival, dressed in all my hippie clothes and my silly hat, etc, and my father had arranged to meet me at ten o'clock outside the entry to the ... the rock festival. But at ten o'clock the best group played – the group was Genesis. So ten o'clock came and I thought 'I'm not going to go home', and I didn't. So I arrived home at about one o'clock in the morning, after a fantastic rock festival with my parents worried, etc. And the next morning my father, who was very, very angry with me, burn ... made a fire in the garden and burned all my hippie clothes ... my hippie trousers, my ... my ... my silly hat, my velvet jacket, etc, and the next day ... even worse ... my mother took me shopping in the ... the local department store and bought me a little, horrible little black and white suit, a little jacket and a little skirt, which is absolutely nothing like hippies wore. I hated them.

Unit 5, Lesson 3, Activities 2 and 3

Interviewer: Can you tell me about some family customs in Italy? How do you see the role of the mother for example?

Ida: Ah, well, the roles are generally very fixed, the male and female roles. The father usually goes out to work and the mother usually stays at home and does the cooking and the ironing and the washing. Very fixed, even though in some cases things are beginning to change.

Interviewer: How are the children expected to behave?

Ida: At home generally the boy has more freedom than the girl. The girl has to ask permission all the time. If she goes out she's accompanied there. They pick her up. They take her home. Boys generally have more freedom, yes.

Interviewer: And what do people think about unmarried couples living together?

Ida: Oh, well, it's not accepted. It's not part of family life. People usually live at home until they get married and then they go and live their separate lives, oh, but you, you just don't live together before you get married.

Interviewer: Is marriage still very popular then?

Ida: Oh, yes. In the south people normally get married quite young ... perhaps twenty, twenty one, and they have children almost immediately. In the north they tend to wait a bit longer ... about twenty five. Yes, marriage is quite popular.

Interviewer: And what's the attitude to divorce?

Ida: Well, people rarely get divorced. It's a Catholic country and the family is very, very important so they generally stay together and try to work things out.

Interviewer: Are there many single parents?

Ida: No, not that I know of. As I said before, the family is very important, so if you are a single parent, you would probably live with your family, the mother and the father.

Interviewer: And what happens to very old relatives when they need to be looked after?

Ida: Well it is sometimes a bit of a problem, really. Unfortunately, for example, grandmothers and grandfathers usually live at home with the family. It can often be very difficult. Very difficult. They never like to send them to old people's homes, because they don't really exist and they don't put them in hospitals or anything like that. They have to stay with the family.

Unit 5, Lesson 3, Activity 4

Interviewer: Jan, can you tell me about family customs in Norway? For example what's the role of the mother?

Jan: Well, I feel it's changed a lot. The roles between father and mother have exchanged in many ways. So you do find a lot of women in Norway ... particularly in the cities ... who work, and the father stays at home looking after the children. You do get traditional couples, but they're often older. In the younger generation there is a lot of interchange now.

Interviewer: And how are children expected to behave at home?

Jan: The family in Norway is quite a liberal unit, and there isn't the sort of problem of discipline that perhaps you have in other countries. If a child does something bad, rather than hitting the child, the child might be talked to, but I don't think there's this kind of discipline problem that you have in more conservative families.

Interviewer: What do people think about living together ... living together before marriage?

Jan: Oh it's totally acceptable. Norway is a Protestant country and many of the people, I think take religion fairly lightly ... but no ... it's totally acceptable to live with a girlfriend and be unmarried.

Interviewer: And is marriage still popular?

Jan: It is popular, but there is a growing percentage of the population who are now unmarried ... and ... er this is quite accepted in society. And a lot of single mothers have good jobs in business or in industry.

Interviewer: Are there many single fathers?

Jan: No ... that's ... there are a few, but I would say it's an insignificant number.

Interviewer: What's the attitude to divorce?

Jan: There's a lot of divorce in Norway. I would say one in two marriages, after four or five years breaks up, so, yes ... and it's also on the increase.

Interviewer: What happens to old relatives when they need to be looked after?

Jan: Well, in rural communities they are almost always looked after by the family ... yes ... because they are quite traditional. But in the city, it can be rather a different story. It could be said to be a sad story. People sometimes reject their grandparents and even their parents once they get older. So when people get very old they often go to an old people's home and are perhaps visited once a month or something like that.

Unit 6, Lesson 1, Activity 5

Lady Francesca:
We all had dinner together at eight o'clock. My husband didn't look well and I think he was worried about something. After dinner he went into his study to write a letter. That was the last time I saw him alive. You asked me what I was wearing ... well, I was wearing a green dress.

Max de Selles:
Well, as you know, everybody had dinner together. Sir Dennis talked to the Contessa all through dinner. Naturally, Lady Francesca was not very happy about this. We sat eating and drinking for a long time and then after dinner I went to the games room. I was playing cards alone when it happened, an awful business. After all, Sir Dennis and I had known each other for a long time. He was a good friend, but a bad businessman. He often had money problems. At the time he died he owed the bank three million pounds! Three million pounds, now that's a lot of money.

Agnes Johansson:
I designed the dress that Lady Francesca was wearing that night. It was a green dress, green is her favourite colour. I noticed that when she came into the hall the dress was torn and she seemed out of breath. I was wearing green too, I put on a green cardigan to go out onto the terrace. It was cold outside. Later, as you know, Sir Dennis was murdered. I must say that I'm not very sorry ... I never liked him very much.

The Contessa:
I met Sir Dennis in Paris last month and he invited me to the château for the weekend. I was surprised but he seemed so kind ... and, well, so genuine. So I accepted. He also told me he had some information for me about my father. When I told my mother about Sir Dennis's invitation she was very upset and she didn't want me to come, I don't know why.

Unit 6, Lesson 2, Activity 7

And finally, time seemed to stand still at Hollingworth Primary School yesterday when a time capsule was buried in the school grounds. The time capsule was buried at a special ceremony at the village school, which was attended by pupils, teachers and parents. Modern coins, photographs of all the children, a copy of the local newspaper and some information about the school and the village were put inside a special box.

An old time capsule from 1860 was discovered at the school by builders, but when it was opened, the contents were found to be damaged. It contained a broken wine bottle, some Victorian money and a newspaper which was too wet to read.

Unit 6, Lesson 3, Activity 5

Presenter: ... Thank you very much. Good evening and welcome to tonight's show ... As usual we have four contestants answering questions on a chosen topic. Our first contestant tonight is William Murphy from Liverpool with questions on the topic of the Olympic Games. ... So are you ready William?

William: Yes, thanks.

Presenter: Right, first question. Do you know what the word Olympiad means? Is it a) a period of four years between the games? Is it b) an ancient Greek sport or is it c) a type of medal?

TAPESCRIPTS

William: Erm ... well ... erm ... it's not a sport, so I'll have to go for a) a, a period of four years between the games.
Presenter: Question 2. Does the host country always come first in the procession at the opening ceremony?
William: Er ... no, I think it comes last. Yeah, yes, it always comes last.
Presenter: Question 3 ... can you tell me how many countries the athletes represent? Is it a) 90, b) 120 or c) more than 140?
William: Well, er ... a lot ... so it's got to be b or c. I'll say more than 140, that's c.
Presenter: On to number 4. Do you know where Carl Lewis won four Olympic gold medals? Was it in a) Barcelona, b) Seoul or c) Los Angeles?
William: Hah ... oh that's easy – Seoul.
Presenter: Question number 5. Are the Olympic medals solid gold?
William: Um ... I'm not sure ... Er ... yes, yes I think so.
Presenter: Six. Which five sports make up the modern pentathlon? Choose from the following: swimming, pistol shooting, long jump, running, fencing, horse-riding, canoeing or gymnastics.
William: Erm ...
Presenter: Shall I say the list again?
William: No, no it's OK. Erm ... let me see ... Er ... I think it's canoeing, erm ... running, fencing, er ... horse-riding and erm ... er ... pistol shooting.
Presenter: Moving on to question number 7. Does the UN, the United Nations, choose the host city for the Olympic games?
William: No, erm ... the International Olympic Committee does.
Presenter: Can you tell me ... this is question number 8 ... can you tell me when Moscow hosted the Olympic games? Was it a) 1980, b) 1984 or c) 1988?
William: 1984.
Presenter: No hesitation there. And now for your last question. Number 9 ... no Olympic games were held in 1914, 1940 and 1944. Why not?
William: Erm ... well, I imagine it's because of the First and Second World Wars.
Presenter: So, that's the end of the questions. Let's have a look at the answers and see how well you did.

Unit 6, Lesson 3, Activity 6

Presenter: Well, your first answer you said a period of years between Olympics and that's correct. Number 2 is in fact true, the host team comes first. You were right with number 3, the answer is more than 140 and number 4 is also correct ... Carl Lewis won all those medals in Seoul. Number 5, I ... I'm afraid you were wrong there William, ... in fact the medals are only gold-plated. And number 6, this was a tricky one, the five sports which make up the modern pentathlon are fencing, swimming, shooting, running and riding. Hah, hah ... you were so close! You just missed out on swimming. Now question 7. You were quite right here. It's the International Olympic Committee who choose the host city for the Olympics, not the UN. And for number 8 ... although you sounded very sure with 1984, it was actually 1980.
William: Oh ... of course.
Presenter: Yes, I knew you knew really. Anyway the last question was right. There were no Olympics in these years because of the world wars.
So, at the end of your round of questions you've scored five out of nine. Well, it's not brilliant, but they were tough questions. We'll have to see how the other contestants get on. So, thank you William, and can we have our next contestant, please?

Unit 7, Lesson 1, Activities 3 and 4

Interviewer: So Sandra, tell me what ... what do you collect?
Sandra: I collect anything to do with aeroplanes ... anything. For example knives and forks, erm ... sugar ... posters ... anything. I've already collected more than a hundred things.
Interviewer: How did it all start?
Sandra: Well, it all started when I came here to, er ... Ecuador because the airport is in the centre of town and I can see all the planes landing and taking off. I can see them from my balcony. And the first thing I collected was some toothpaste ... some Viasa toothpaste. And, er ... now I'm obsessed.
Interviewer: And do you like flying, yourself?
Sandra: No, I hate it! ... I get paranoid when I fly ... It really frightens me.
Interviewer: Oh ... I see. Well, that's strange! You said you started your collection when you came here ... when was that exactly?
Sandra: About four years ago. And now, of course all my friends and colleagues know about my collection so they all bring me things. Someone in fact gave me a luggage label this morning ... some luggage labels they'd got. And ... and look ... I've also just got this shoe horn ... that's quite unusual. A friend's just sent it from Hong Kong.
Interviewer: A shoe horn. Yes, that is unusual. So, what is your favourite thing in your collection?
Sandra: Well, the best thing is my Lufthansa scarf. I've had that for about a year now. I just saw a pilot wearing one in the airport one day and I just went up to him, told him about my collection and asked if I could have it. And he took it off and gave it to me. So now I've got that on the wall. That's definitely the best thing so far.
Interviewer: And where do you keep all these things?
Sandra: In my spare bedroom. I've turned it into an airport waiting lounge. It's got model aeroplanes suspended from the ceiling and posters on the wall. Though all the knives and forks and things like that are in the kitchen.
Interviewer: What airlines have you collected things from?
Sandra: Well, Lufthansa, as I said, and Air France, Iberia ... Egypt Air ... in fact my most unusual spoon is from that airline. I got that from an old work colleague about a year ago.
Interviewer: So what would you really like to have now for your collection?
Sandra: Well, I haven't got much from any African airlines yet – so that would be nice, but what I'd really like ... well, I suppose what I'd like most would be a pilot's hat or some piece of uniform, but that would be very difficult to get ... very difficult.
Interviewer: Well, I'll try my best next time I fly!

Unit 7, Lesson 2, Activity 2

1
Interviewer: Excuse me. Could you spare a moment to answer a few questions about your school?
Girl: My school. OK ... um ... but I've been to several.
Interviewer: Well, where do you go to school at the moment?
Girl: Well, it's a girl's school ... yes, an all-girls school.
Interviewer: How long have you been going there?
Girl: About a year.
Interviewer: I see. And, um, how many subjects do you study?
Girl: Ten or eleven at the moment.
Interviewer: And which are your favourite subjects?
Girl: Favourite subjects ... Oh ... don't really have any (laugh) erm ... History and erm ... English I suppose.
Interviewer: Okay. Thank you very much.

2
Interviewer: Good morning. Sorry to disturb you, but would you mind answering a few questions?
Man: Well, I'm in rather a hurry.
Interviewer: It, it won't take long. You see, we're doing some market research about television viewing habits. So we'd like to know what sort of things you watch.
Man: OK, but it'll have to be quick.
Interviewer: To start with, how much TV do you usually watch a week?
Man: Oh, I don't know ... probably about twenty hours, I think.
Interviewer: And how much TV have you watched this week?
Man: Well I've been watching more than usual because I'm off work, so, say, about 25.
Interviewer: And, and what sort of programmes do you like? What's your favourite type of TV programme?
Man: Oh, comedy shows, and detective series ... well, most things.
Interviewer: Um ... just one last question ...

3
Interviewer: Excuse me ... er, excuse me, sir, may I just ask a few questions? We're doing a survey for the leisure services on people's interests. So, I was wondering if you could tell me about what you do in your free time?
Man: Er ... well, I've not got much free time, but I like going to the cinema if there's a good film on, and, and football ... well, I prefer watching it rather than playing. But I spend most of my free time collecting bottles.
Interviewer: Oh! So, that's your main leisure interest?
Man: Yeah, yes, I suppose it is.
Interviewer: How long have you been collecting bottles? When did you start?
Man: Oh, erm ... well, I suppose I've been collecting for about ten years. I've probably collected over 300 by now.
Interviewer: And when do you find time to collect?
Man: Well, mainly at weekends ...

4
Interviewer: Sorry, ... excuse me, madam, could you spare a few minutes? I'm doing some market research for the new passenger service. Have you just come off one of our flights?
Woman: Yes, I have.

70

TAPESCRIPTS

Interviewer: And did you fly first class, business class or tourist class?
Woman: Tourist class ... it was expensive enough as it was.
Interviewer: Right. Well, er, could I ...
Woman: I mean, I wouldn't mind, but I've been travelling with your company since you started and the prices just keep going up and up.
Interviewer: Erm ... yes, well, er ... what did you think of the food and the cabin crew, etc?
Woman: Well, it wasn't one of the best flights I've been on, but I suppose the food was OK, but the seats were uncomfortable ... and ... and then there was the heating and ...

Unit 7, Lesson 3, Activity 4

... and just before we go over to the weather centre I have just received a police message concerning a missing person.
Police are looking for a Miranda Grey, an art student at the Slade School of Art.
She went missing last night, some time between about six and eight o'clock. She rang her home in Hampstead, North London some time just before six to say that she would be going to the cinema because it was raining, but that she would be home just after eight. The call was made from a nearby station and police fear that she may have disappeared somewhere between the cinema and her home. Miranda is twenty years old. She's about five foot four inches tall. She's slim and she's got long blonde hair. She was wearing a blue jumper and a white blouse and a dark green skirt.
If you saw anyone answering this description between six and eight pm, please contact your local police station.
Once again, that's a twenty-year-old art student, Miranda Grey, who is missing from home. Please let the police know if you think you have seen her.
And now we'll go over to the weather centre, as promised, for the latest forecast ...

Unit 8, Lesson 1, Activity 3

Suzie: Hey, the International festival starts this weekend!
Brian: Oh yeah.
Suzie: Sorry I disturbed you!
Geoff: Never mind him. What's on? I fancy going out next week 'cos I'm off work.
Suzie: Well, it starts with a dinner and folk dancing on Sunday. How about going to the dinner?
Geoff: OK, fine. I haven't been out to eat in ages. Here, Brian even you should be interested in that.
Brian: Er ... yeah, yeah sure.
Suzie: Shall we go then, Brian?
Brian: [grunts]
Geoff: I think that means yes. And let's go to a club or something afterwards.
Suzie: I'd prefer to go Scottish dancing. It's on the programme for Monday. How about that?
Brian: Hey, yeah, yeah ... great idea. It would be good for a laugh.
Geoff: I'm sorry I can't. I'm playing chess on Monday.
Brian: Oh well, I still fancy going dancing though.
Suzie: Well, there's a Samba band playing at the City Hall on Saturday. Huh ... that would be good to dance to. Why don't we all go there?
Geoff: Yeah, that's great. Saturday's no problem. Brian?
Brian: Yeah, yeah ... I'm free then.
Geoff: And ... er ... shall we go to the cinema one night?
Suzie: Well, I'd prefer to do something different – we can see a film anytime.
Geoff: Oh, alright. Well, what about the Moscow acrobats? That's something different. They're on Thursday.
Suzie: Excellent. Shall I get three tickets then?
Brian: I'm afraid I can't come. I'm playing tennis.
Suzie: Come on Brian. Can't you play some other time?
Geoff: Yeah, come on Brian.
Brian: Oh … OK, yeah, I guess I can rearrange it. Let's see the acrobats. You sh ... you can get three tickets.
Geoff: Have you seen there's a Tai Chi talk? You were talking about taking that up, weren't you?
Suzie: Well, hah ... I was thinking about it.
Geoff: So why don't you go and find out more about it?
Suzie: Um ... perhaps ... Brian ...are you interested in coming?
Brian: Ah ... not really. I'd prefer to do something more active ... But you go and you can tell me what I've missed.
Geoff: Mmm … there really is lots on. Going back to Saturday ... why don't we watch the fireworks before we go to the Samba band? So that's agreed then? Right, now that we've sorted out our social life for next week, let's have something to eat. How about some spaghetti?
Brian: Hah, hah ... fine, I'll come and give you a hand.

Unit 8, Lesson 1, Activity 4

1
Suzie: Well it starts with a dinner and folk dancing on Sunday. How about going to the dinner?
Geoff: OK, fine.

2
Geoff: And let's go to a club or something afterwards.
Suzie: I'd prefer to go Scottish dancing. It's on the programme for Monday. How about that?
Brian: Hey, yeah, yeah ... great idea. It would be good for a laugh.
Geoff: I'm sorry, I can't. I'm playing chess on Monday.

3
Geoff: And ... er ... shall we go to the cinema one night.
Suzie: Well, I'd prefer to do something different – we can see a film anytime.
Geoff: Oh, alright. Well, what about the Moscow acrobats?

Unit 8, Lesson 2, Activities 3 and 4

Good evening to you all and welcome. Thank you all very much for coming. I'm looking forward to showing you some of my slides and telling you about my adventures in Iceland. Please feel free to stop me ... and ... er ... ask any questions as we go along.
Right. ... now this first slide shows a map of Iceland, which is one of the most active volcanic areas in the world. It lies in the Atlantic Ocean, just outside the Arctic Circle. The line across the top there is the Arctic Circle, which touches the northern tip of the island. Because I was this far north and it was summer I had almost twenty four hours daylight to walk in. I set off on foot across Iceland on June the twenty-third, 1984. To the right, on the east coast is the small town of Seydisfjordur, where I started my journey. From there I walked 510 miles across to the west coast so that's ... about ... er ... 800 kilometres. The journey took me 24 days to complete.
Now, before I give you a detailed account of the walk, I'd like to show you a few slides just to give you an idea of some of the sorts of things that happened. Well, here I am on Vatnajokull, which is the largest glacier in Iceland. In fact, it's larger than all the other glaciers of Europe put together. It really is enormous ... over 1000 metres thick in places. It was a really dangerous climb, partly because I ... I did it on my own, and also because it was the first time I'd done any ice climbing. In fact, just after I took this photo I fell about 50 metres, which nearly killed me. But ... er ... more of that later.
Well, er ... from the freezing cold glacier to the steaming hot volcano. This is me on the climb up to Mount Hekla, which last erupted in 1981, so when I was there it was still very much an active volcano, and I did in fact burn myself. See that ... er ... mark there on my leg ... well that's the burn mark.
This is a particularly dangerous river, which flows down from one of the glaciers. As you can see the water is very fast, and of course it's freezing cold. I had to cross several rivers like this. Another problem I had was navigation. Although I had a good up-to-date map, which I'd bought in Reykjavik, the ... the land ... as you can see.. is well very difficult.. a black desert of volcanic ash, where there are no plants, animals or people, and where there are no roads or tracks, so that I often got lost. I also got very hungry because there was no wood to use to light a fire to cook on. I realize now it was stupid not to take dried food, but at the time I didn't think about it.
So, here I am very thin, hungry and, erm ... tired at the end of my journey.
Anyway ... so ... er ... that gives you an idea of what the journey was like and now I'll ... er ... yes, sorry. You have a question ... yes, what would you like to ask?

Unit 8, Lesson 3, Activity 2

Chair: Okay ... right, good evening everyone. Are we ready to start the meeting? First on the agenda is the festival programme. Tonight we need to choose some events for the festival. I'd like to ask Jerry ... in charge of music ... to tell us his news first.
Jerry: Well, first let me give you news of the pop group situation …
Liz: Oh no I really don't think a pop group's a good idea.
Martin: Oh, I do, I think ...
Chair: Wait a moment, let Jerry finish.
Jerry: Well, it looks too expensive ... erm ... yes, they're going to be expensive and the town hall is ... erm ... too small.
Chair: I'm not so sure about that, I mean ...
Martin: Yeah ... I don't think the town hall's too small.
Liz: Well, I do.

71

TAPESCRIPTS

Jerry: Anyway, could I just finish? I've been looking into the possibility of a local jazz group called 'Saxophone'.
Liz: Oh, now that's a great idea. They're really popular.
Martin: Yeah, that sounds fine. I love jazz.
Chair: Mmm … so do I. Anyway … so, no pop group, but we're having a jazz group. Right, let's move on to sport. Rita, could you tell us about the sport situation?
Rita: Well, we think a five-a-side football competition is the best idea. People are very interested …
Jerry: Sorry, could I just say something here? I don't think this is a good idea.
Liz: Neither do I because I don't …
Jerry: Because we've nowhere to play football.
Liz: Yes, Jerry's right. We've … we've no decent pitch.
Chair: OK then. But we'll need to come up with another idea for sport. Martin, what's happening with the Greek folk group? Are they coming?
Martin: Yeah, they are and that's really good … something different.
Jerry: Yes, something different and really spectacular. I've seen them.
Liz: Good, good …
Chair: Fine. So we agree on that? Right, next item.. the art exhibition … Who's organizing that?
Liz: Oh, I am, actually. Er … we thought of having er … a children's art exhibition … we thought it was a good idea to get the children involved.
Rita: Oh, I agree. And the parents will like it.
Chair: Excellent. Let's move on to the lecture and slide show on Mount Everest. Jerry?
Jerry: Could we put that off to the next meeting because I've got no news at the moment?
Chair: OK, so we'll leave that for the moment. Has anybody got anything else to say?
Martin: Yes, we need to discuss the fancy-dress disco.
Jerry: Oh no, Oh, I'm not keen on fancy-dress. I mean, I think it's too difficult to get costumes.
Liz: Yes, so do I. Oh, it's too difficult. Costs too much money.
Martin: Yeah I agree. it's far too difficult to … and it takes too much time to make a fancy-dress. I think most people would prefer a normal disco.
Chair: Mmm … I think you're right there. Well, let's say no to the fancy-dress because of the problem of costume, and we'll put off the decision about the Mount Everest talk until next week. And we need to talk about the celebrity golf match. OK? I think that's all we need to discuss tonight. So let's decide a date for the next meeting.

Unit 9, Lesson 1, Activity 6

Interviewer: Ms Darracott, are you there?
Ms Darracott: Hello, yes.
Interviewer: And can you hear me?
Ms Darracott: Yes certainly.
Interviewer: Well, could you tell us please. What's your opinion of whaling?
Ms Darracott: Well, I don't see any harm in it frankly. I think a lot of people depend on it for their jobs, for their whole livelihood.
Interviewer: Oh, right, well, Mr Dominic Strowbridge, our other caller. Do you agree with Ms Darracott?
Mr Strowbridge: I strongly disagree. Whales are facing extinction because of this indiscriminate killing.
Ms Darracott: Oh, come on – a little extreme. The situation isn't as bad as that.
Mr Strowbridge: Oh, but it is. There are certain countries which have not signed this international ban on whaling, and the number of Blue Whales and Sperm Whales is dropping dramatically.
Ms Darracott: But a lot of people depend … I mean cultures for centuries have depended on whales.
Mr Strowbridge: But if you keep going on whaling, killing the whales so fast then there won't be any jobs for these people. And besides, whales are so important for the control of the environment. They keep the numbers of fish down.
Ms Darracott: But they're important for medicine too.
Mr Strowbridge: But it's not only medicine. We can learn so much from whales because …
Interviewer: Yes, but …
Mr Strowbridge: No, please don't interrupt. Whales are the second most intelligent animals after humans …
Ms Darracott: I still think …
Interviewer: Sorry to interrupt you there, but I don't think we've got any more time. Thank you both very much. Next caller please.

Unit 9, Lesson 2, Activity 5

1
Well, let's see. It's, um … long, very thin, doesn't have any legs. Um, often, it's … it's got a long tongue also. Let's see. Um … usually it's … it's a dangerous animal, you don't want to get close to it. It's poisonous. Um … what kind of skin does it have? It's got very smooth skin. What else? It lives in … I think it usually lives in the grass.

2
They're quite hairy, and some have a long tail. They have long arms and they look a bit like humans. They live in trees and they are really agile. They can make a lot of noise and they eat nuts and fruit.

3
Well, it's a bird, but it can't fly. It's black and white and it's really funny. It walks from side to side. It swims and mainly lives in Antarctica.

4
Well, it's got four legs and it's got a long tail. It's got a fairly long head, looks like a donkey. It's got a mane, lives in Africa, and eats grass, and it's black and white.

5
Well, it's very, very big and grey with big floppy ears, quite short legs, lives in Africa and India. In India it can be used for transportation, but in Africa it's wild. Oh and, and it has a long trunk.

Unit 9, Lesson 3, Activity 3

Anthony: Um … well, let's see. It was a few years ago, I suppose. Um … we were on an island er … down in the South of the Philippines, right down by the Equator. It was very, very primitive. Um … we were staying in a hut on the beach. Um … I was with my girlfriend. I remember it was right at the end of the hot season. It was too hot to do anything. Um … the temperature was up in the hundreds every day. Anyway, one night we were woken up … um … I suppose it must have been about two or three o'clock in the morning, by the sound of wind … um … in the trees and very, very heavy rain on the roof. And what was strange was that we could feel the hut being lifted up and er … er … the walls moving. Anyway we, we got up and we, we turned the light on and opened the door. We looked out, but it was … the rain was er … too heavy to see very much... and er … we could see, we could see that the sea was … was high up the beach and er … the waves were were, huge … huge great waves. Um … the sky was, was quite light because there was er … there was a full moon, and we could see the clouds racing, racing across the skies. The wind … the wind was very strong and the … all the palm trees were, were swaying and some of them were …were falling. Um … suddenly the lights went out, there was, er … a power cut so the electricity had gone. Um … I don't know …half of me felt terrified, um … but my girlfriend was laughing and er … half of me was enjoying it. We just … we just stayed there watching the storm until morning. Um … the beach was covered in rubbish – wood, leaves, everything … um … the next morning, but it was … it was very quiet and er … and the sky was blue again. Very strange.

Unit 10, Lesson 2, Activities 3 and 4

Interviewer: So, Eric, can you tell us about your bike ride? When did you start?
Eric: Well, Lina and I began our journey in August 1990 at Lake Titicaca, outside La Paz in Bolivia.
Interviewer: And how long did you spend there?
Eric: Oh, about two months, at a very high altitude … about 4,000 metres above sea level. We cycled through mountainous countryside and across salt flats … vast salt flats and …
Interviewer: And after Bolivia?
Eric: Well, after about two months in Bolivia we crossed into Chile and went from over 4,000 metres above sea level down to the coast … lovely beaches. Then, from there we travelled 700 kilometres across the driest desert in the world – the Atacama desert – to Santiago.
Interviewer: Did you stop and rest anywhere?
Eric: Yes, we stopped in Santiago, the capital city of Chile, for a month.
Interviewer: How long were you in Chile for altogether?
Eric: For about four months.
Interviewer: What was the countryside like?
Eric: Well, very varied … I mean, after Santiago we cycled through the wine-growing region, lots of vineyards. Then we moved on through the forests of southern Chile to the Lake District. That's where it got really exciting. We cycled past glaciers and saw them crashing into lakes and huge … oh, huge mountains covered in forests.
Interviewer: That must have been amazing. So you … um … spent four months in Chile and then?
Eric: And then we had to zig-zag in and out of Chile and Argentina, so we probably spent about a month in Argentina, finishing in Ushuaia, the southern-most town in the world.
Interviewer: When did you arrive there?
Eric: End of February 1991.
Interviewer: So how far did you cycle?
Eric: In total, 4,200 miles, that's 6,700 kilometres.
Interviewer: That's amazing. And that took you seven months?
Eric: Yeah, that's right.
Interviewer: Well, it sounds a fascinating

experience. You must write a book about your trip, I'd love to read it!

Unit 10, Lesson 2, Activity 8

Interviewer: So tell me, Eric, what was the best moment on your trip?

Eric: I suppose the highlight of the whole trip was camping near this glacier in southern Argentina, where the ice was the height of about a ten-storey building, and just watching the whole thing crash into a lake. The waves, the ice ... I think that was probably the best moment.

Interviewer: And your worst moment?

Eric: Um ... I suppose the worst moment was when we had a mechanical problem. We were 80 miles from nowhere in the middle of this plateau in Argentina. Very bad winds, about 100 kilometres per hour ... something like that ... and Lina's bike broke down. And we had a lot of trouble getting to civilisation.

Interviewer: And overall, what was your biggest fear throughout the trip?

Eric: I think the biggest fear was having problems with people if they wouldn't accept us, or something like that. You know, being robbed ... that kind of thing ... much more than the physical element.

Interviewer: Right, OK. So, finally, what about the future?

Eric: My dream, my ambition would be to cycle across central Asia. That would be Mongolia, Tibet and then cycle along the Himalayas and probably end up in Pakistan.

Interviewer: And when do you hope to do that?

Eric: Probably in four or five years time. We must save up some money first!